MARYLAND AND DISTRICT OF COLUMBIA VOLUNTEERS IN THE MEXICAN WAR

Charles J. Wells

HERITAGE BOOKS
2008

HERITAGE BOOKS
AN IMPRINT OF HERITAGE BOOKS, INC.

Books, CDs, and more—Worldwide

For our listing of thousands of titles see our website
at
www.HeritageBooks.com

Published 2008 by
HERITAGE BOOKS, INC.
Publishing Division
100 Railroad Ave. #104
Westminster, Maryland 21157

Copyright © 1991 Charles J. Wells

All rights reserved. No part of this book may be reproduced or transmitted in any form or by any means, electronic or mechanical, including photocopying, recording or by any information storage and retrieval system without written permission from the author, except for the inclusion of brief quotations in a review.

International Standard Book Numbers
Paperbound: 978-0-940907-19-5
Clothbound: 978-0-7884-7069-1

To My Wife

Deany

Acknowledgements

The research and writing of this book would not have been possible without the assistance and encouragement of many friends, colleagues, and members of my family. I wish to thank the Mr. Bill Lind and Mr. Michael Meier of the National Archives for their time and outstanding help in locating and making available the muster rolls of the battalion and regiment. Ms. Theresa McGill of the Chicago Historical Society was most cooperative in providing copies of a manuscript within days of my request. The Staff of the Baltimore City Archives, which led me to Watson's monument on Mount Royal and North Avenues, provided excellent support during my visits. Finally to Mr. Henry Peden, Jr., an old friend from college days, I thank for his advice and proffering of information on short notice.

Table of Contents

Introduction: How to Use This Book vii
Map: The Seat of War ix
History of the Maryland and DC Volunteers 1
Compendium of Volunteers 12
Muster Roll for the Baltimore and
    District of Columbia Battalion 79
Muster Roll for the Maryland and
    District of Columbia Regiment 84
Recruiting Party 89

Introduction: How to Use This Book

The information used to develop this book was derived from many different sources. The brief history is based upon J.R. Kenly's <u>Memoirs of a Volunteer in the War With Mexico</u> and, unless otherwise noted, follows his diary. The compilation of volunteers that served in the Maryland and District of Columbia units is based primarily on the muster rolls and Mexican War Pension Lists located in the United States National Archives. Does this book list all Maryland and D.C. residents who participated in the Mexican War? It does not. Not included are residents who served in the regular army and navy of the United States or volunteered in regiments of neighboring states. This listing contains only those individuals classified as volunteers in the battalion and regiment raised in Maryland and the District of Columbia. All information in the following format was derived from those sources unless otherwise stated in the listing:

Soldier's name: As in working with official records from the U.S. Censuses, the researcher must be careful when searching for a particular individual. The spelling of names is totally dependent upon the literacy of the recorder of that information. For example, on one muster roll a soldier named "Connelly" was listed as "Conili." Other such examples abound. When searching, think of other spellings for that individual's name.

Rank: Unless stated, all soldiers are privates.

Unit: Some soldiers served in more than one unit. I have attempted to list other units when that information is available. Unfortunately, few muster rolls exist for some units.

City: This entry is the city or place of enlistment. Generally, a soldier enlisted in a city or unit that was near his home.

Age and Date: The age provided is as of the date provided in parenthesis.

Remarks: Comments are derived from numerous sources. If no source is listed then the information was obtained from the muster rolls. All pension-related information is derived from the Index to the Mexican War Pension Files, 1887-1926, Microfilm T-317. All other information is keyed to the following list of sources: (Complete descriptions of the references can be found in the bibliography)

A = The Mexican War and Its Warriors - J. Frost
B = Baltimore Sun
C = Baltimore City Directory
D = McCulloch's Texas Rangers
E = Baltimore Sunday Herald
F = Who Was Who in the Union
G = National Archives Pension Records Index
H = History of the Mexican War - C. Wilcox
J = Daily Republican Argus

Introduction: How to Use This Book

K = Memoirs of a Maryland Volunteer - J.R. Kenly
L = Records of the Association of Mexican War Veterans
M = Tercentenary History of Maryland
N = National Intelligencer
O = Biographical Cyclopedia
P = History and Roster of Maryland Volunteers (Union), War of 1861-65, Vol.1
Q = Baltimore American
R = Maryland Historical Society - Manuscript Collection
W = Washington City Directory

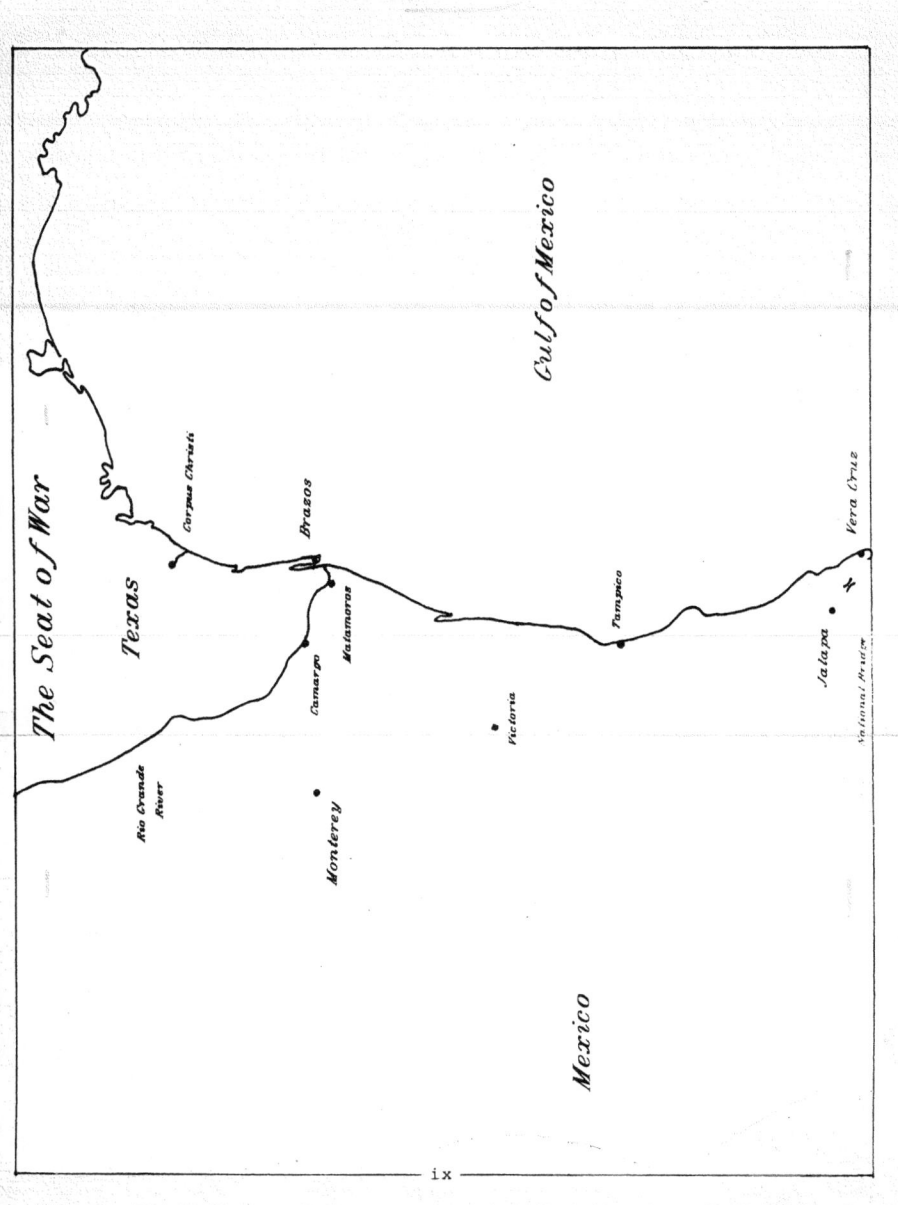

History of the Maryland and District of Columbia Volunteers

Call to Arms: The Baltimore and Washington Battalion of Volunteers

By May of 1846, the United States and Mexico had moved to the brink of war. General Zachary Taylor had formed and moved his army south to the Rio Grande and was preparing to move further inland. President Polk, describing the atrocities committed by the Mexicans against neighboring Texas, presented a strong argument to the people and Congress to enter into America's first foreign war. Despite the pacifist sentiments of several Northern legislators, Congress acceded and formally declared war against Mexico on May 16, 1846. The War Bill called upon each state to raise volunteers for one year service in Mexico.

In Maryland the response was swift. Governor Pratt, as chief of the state's militia, called for the formation of two regiments from Maryland. The military organizations and clubs that had existed since the end of the War of 1812 became the basis for the recruiting of many companies. As early as May 13th, militia leaders gathered in Monument Square to rally citizens for duty in the service of General Zachary Taylor in Mexico.[1] Baltimore responded by organizing four companies with names such as the Chesapeake Riflemen, Baltimore's Own, and the President's Guards. Training for these bakers, millers, watermen, and printers was provided by the existing militia units such as the Eagle Artillery. Captain Steuart marched his company through the streets of Baltimore and began drilling at Howard's Park, near the corner of Madison and Calvert Streets.[2]

The nation's capital also began organizing volunteers. In the 1830's the militia organization in Washington City had declined to a small band of determined enthusiasts. In the late 1830's, recruitment improved enabling the formation of the Washington Light Infantry Company. It probably was this unit which formed the basis for the volunteer companies active in 1845. After a City Hall meeting on May 15, 1846, Washington Volunteer Company, Number 1, was established electing John Waters as captain, William Parham as first lieutenant, and Eugene Boyle as second lieutenant. A second company, the Washington City Riflemen, was formed several days later electing officers, Robert Bronaugh, Phineas B. Bell, and William O'Brien.[3]

The companies, six in number, now formed the Baltimore and Washington Battalion of Volunteers. The military advisor to the Governor of Maryland, Colonel William Watson, was appointed a lieutenant colonel of volunteers and commander of the battalion. Ordered to Washington, D.C. in the first week of June, the four companies from Baltimore were quartered at the Marine Barracks awaiting the two companies from that city. By June 10th, the Secretary of War issued orders for the battalion to relocate south near Fort Washington. Embarkation would occur at this location vice the City of Washington. Apparently the mayor of Washington was eager to have the men depart the city. Several men from Baltimore were rowdy and in at least one instance were returned to the unit by the local constabulary. On June 13th, the unit was ferried to the steamer *Massachusetts*, lying in the Potomac River. Preparations for the journey aboard the steamer continued for three days.

The voyage to Point Isabel at the mouth of the Rio Grande, then part of Mexico, would prove to be arduous and costly. On June 16th, the steamer began its journey down the river to the Chesapeake Bay and beyond. During the voyage, the officers were forced to suppress several fights, quarrels, and general rioting of the troops. Rum and other alcoholic drinks were the major culprits during the long nights at sea. Near the Florida Keys, the steamer bounced off the bottom several times as it neared the reefs. Several more storms, the heat, and a lack of water would contribute to more difficulties during the journey. Finally, on July 1st, the island of Brazos, off the coast of Texas, came into view for the weary volunteers. Brazos was General Taylor's staging port for the volunteer regiments joining the American army.

Mexico

John Reese Kenly had always been interested in military affairs since his youth. At an early age, he joined a military club and began training throughout his school years. The decision to volunteer and become captain of a company was not difficult. His memoirs of life in the battalion provide an excellent view of the war from a volunteer and Marylander. Captain Kenly's first reports of life in Mexico were not encouraging. On the small barrier island, shade and water were in short supply. Volunteers from Missouri, Tennessee, Alabama, Mississippi, and Louisiana were also awaiting orders in the transient camps. The number of troops in this small area over-extended the island's capability to supply the large force. With trees for shade lacking, the troops bathed in the inviting surf of the Gulf of Mexico. Unfortunately, Kenly's first casualty would occurred on the island. Richard Belt of Carroll County was drowned while bathing during a day when the surf was extremely rough.

The march inland began on July 9, 1846. Unfortunately for the men of the Baltimore Battalion, the march ended after several miles as the volunteers were ordered to make camp near the delta of the Rio Grande until the advance could continue. This delay would be remembered because of the mosquitoes, the heat and the humidity. On July 23rd, the battalion marched to the small town of Burita and established a camp on the chaparral. Although it may have been a welcomed change from the delta it was a new camp fraught with rattlesnakes and wild cattle. Quarreling erupted among the troops. An incident occurred on the 23rd between the 1st Ohio Regiment and the Baltimore Battalion. An argument began over some catfish caught in the river by troopers of the Baltimore Battalion; with the use of Ohio fishing tackle. The colonel of the Ohio unit reportedly slashed an enlisted man of the Baltimore unit and attempted to steal the fish. Upon this news, several companies of the battalion formed up and prepared to do battle with the buckeyes. Only common sense and cool headed officers managed to calm the troops and discuss the problem with the Ohio Colonel. Allen Paine, a regular soldier from Baltimore in the 3rd Infantry Regiment, recorded in his diary that the regulars were called out to separate the two groups.[4] The volunteers' restlessness was exhibited by similar events occurring between other volunteer regiments along the Rio Grande. General Taylor acted as arbitrator and with some trepidation ordered the volunteers to prepare for the march to Camargo.

The Baltimore and Washington Battalion of Volunteers had established a reputation for rowdiness and disorder. While awaiting the S.S. Massachusetts in Alexandria, Virginia, many of the unit's troops had to be returned to ship by the local constabulary for drunkenness and disturbing the peace. When Colonel Watson formed the unit, he took great pains to ensure that the unit's uniform would be the same dark blue as the regulars. Many of the other volunteers' units had used more creative uniforms varying in color and design. The Baltimoreans tended to taunt the other units about their uniforms adding further to their reputation.

The order came to march. On the morning of August 7th, the companies of Captains Steuart and Waters prepared to board a steamer for Camargo. The four remaining companies were to march west four days later. Prior to departing, Dr. Love and 33 men of the Battalion were discharged by surgeons certificate and returned to the United States. The Battalion resumed its march westward and reached Matamoras by the 14th. At Matamoras, the Baltimoreans were brigaded with Kentucky and Ohio volunteers and marched for Camargo on the 15th. The journey over the barren and rugged terrain would last eight days.

General Taylor's army camped outside of Camargo awaiting additional supplies. The life of a military officer in the 1840's was not all leadership and adventure. On August 30th, Captain Kenly recounted an event in his memoirs of the difficulty in preparing muster rolls. In his own words is the following account.

"...Orders were received that our battalion would be mustered tomorrow for payment, and that each Captain should have prepared and ready for that day four full rolls containing the names of all the members of his company, present and absent, where mustered, when mustered, when last paid, the amount of clothing each man had received, the value of the equipments, arms, and accoutrements received by each, the amount due the sutler, and a recapitulation showing the number present for duty, those that were present sick, those that were absent sick, those on extra duty, those in arrest or confinement, those on detached service, those absent without leave, the number joined by transfer, the number joined from desertion, the number discharged by expiration of service, or for disability, the number that had

deserted, the number that had died, etc., etc. I looked at the
blank forms, and my military enthusiasm was oozing perceptibly
through my pores. No help for it; the work had to be done. So,
selecting some half-dozen of the best clerks in my company, I
went at it. We labored hard, for no one officer or soldier in
the command had ever had anything of the kind to do before.
Labor as we did, however, I could not make my account balance,--
that is the only way to express it; in other words, I could not
make this roll correspond with the original one made in
Washington on the 8th of June, when we mustered into the
army...."

On September 1st, General Taylor gave the order to march
westward. The Baltimore Battalion, through the efforts of
Colonel Watson, was brigaded with the U.S. First Regiment of
Infantry Regulars under General Twiggs. The first destination
was the town of Seralvo, seventy miles from Camargo. The brigade
arrived on the 9th and began to receive word that General Ampudia
was fortifying the city of Monterey. All indicators pointed to a
fight soon.

The Battle of Monterey

Marching from Seralvo to Monterey, constant rumors of Mexican
lancers concerned the U.S. infantry regiments. McCullough's
Texas Rangers had engaged the lancers on several occasions in the
past days. Kenly's company, acting as the advance party on the
15th moved through a deserted Mexican town and observed the
feared lancers at a distance. Finally on the 19th, Taylor's army
had reached the outskirts of Monterey and settled into camp at
Walnut Springs, a wooded area approximately three miles from the
city.

All day long on the 19th, the initial sounds of battle could
be heard in the distance. Mexican artillery fire from the town
was followed by U.S. artillery into the town. The U.S. cavalry
continued to reconnoiter the defenses of the city and harass the
forts and garrisons. On the 20th, the order came to form into
battle formation and march toward the city. The battalion
marched with the regulars to within sight of the city and stood
there for hours awaiting further orders. None came. The units
marched back to camp for the night.

On the morning of September 21, 1846, Kenly was summoned to
the tent of Colonel Watson. Watson informed Kenly that the
Baltimore Battalion was to join Twigg's Division in the attack on
Monterey this day. Unfortunately one company was to be left
behind as a camp guard, as well as one detail of men from each
company. Captain Bronaugh's Washington company was selected to
remain, much to the chagrin of Bronaugh. With the removal of one
company plus the other guard detail, the Baltimore Battalion was
marching into battle with approximately 230 men.

By 9:00 a.m., the Fourth Brigade had assembled for the attack.
Approaching the city from the north east, the brigade was to

assault the forts guarding the eastern edge of the city as a "demonstration" to confuse the Mexican defenders. While the remainder of Twigg's Division stood in reserve, Worth's Division would conduct the main assault on the city's defenses from the west. Twigg assigned Colonel Garland's 4th Brigade, consisting of the Baltimore Battalion, the 1st and 3rd Infantry Regiments, the task of making the initial assault. The Baltimore Battalion was given the left flank as they moved steadily through a cornfield to within 500 yards of the fort on eastern edge of the city known as the Teneria. The brigade remained in this position for what seemed to be an eternity for the troops. Finally the word to advance was shouted. The following events are in Captain Kenly's own words:

"...We advanced toward the fort with steadiness and rapidity, receiving its fire of round and grape shot, and the musketry of its infantry supports, when there came across our line of advance, and apparently in close proximity, the sound of an eighteen-pound ball sent from the citadel (another fort north of the city). We were being enfiladed! Still we advanced; another shot from the citadel, and the leg of Lieutenant Dilworth of the First Infantry, was taken off as he stepped. ...Still we advanced, notwithstanding this additional fire on our exposed flank, until we were within a little less than one hundred yards of the fort, until two of the guns were abandoned by their gunners, when, just at the moment the fruits of our gallant charge were within or grasp, our brigade commander committed the unpardonable blunder of changing the point of attack, and attempting to move by the right flank by file left, into a street of the town which debouched into the plain, about opposite the right of our line--our battalion being directly in front of the fort on its left. ...the impetus of our charge was gone."

Amidst the chaos, the Mexicans were firing at the American forces from three sides. Sergeant George Herring of Baltimore was knocked over by a volley from the fort. Sergeant John Axer was one of the first to stop and tend to the wounded man. "Go on boys," gasped Herring, "you can not do anything for me, and when you get to Baltimore, tell them I died game."[5] Many regulars and volunteers broke at this point. The 1st and 3rd Regiments moved into the town's streets with the remainder of the Baltimore Battalion following. The Brigade became bogged down in house to house fighting. The Mexicans occupied the roofs of many of the buildings and were putting a horrendous fire on the American infantry. Finally, Colonel Garland, realizing the folly of continuing the battle under these circumstances, gave the order to retreat. Watson asked Kenly which way he was going? Kenly replied, "With the men." Whereupon, the 4th Brigade began its retreat from the city.

The Brigade was now in full flight. As they came into range of the forts surrounding the town, they were fired at again and again until reaching the staging area near the reserve forces. It must be noted that in many accounts of the Battle of Monterey, particularly Ripley's, the Baltimore Battalion was reported to have been broken and routed by the Mexican fire. Many of the troops did break and run.[6] To add to the confusion, the Battalion, as well as the remainder of the Brigade, was ordered to retreat. After the retreat Garland ordered Captain Kenly to rally the Battalion and the regulars to defend the artillery battery of Braxton Bragg against a unit of Mexican Lancers advancing toward the battery's rear. Kenly's group of about 180 officers and men of the Baltimore Battalion successfully forced the Lancers to retreat. The Battalion then advanced to the ramparts of the Teneria, which had been taken by a battalion of regulars while the remainder of the Brigade had assaulted the town, and found shelter from the deadly fire from the town and Fort Diablo. The Baltimore Battalion remained in this position until dusk when the American forces withdrew to the outskirts of the city.

The death of Colonel Watson was one of the great tragedies of the day for the Baltimoreans. After Watson had passed Garland's order to retreat to Kenly, he rode his mount toward the Tanneria near the southeast edge of the city closely followed by Lieutenant Oden Bowie and several men. At this time, men of the 1st Ohio Volunteers were charging into the town in support of the 4th Brigade. Watson joined these men, leading the assault further into the city. In a flash of musket fire from the rooftops, Watson's horse was shot from under him. Still standing, Watson raised his sword to lead the small group against the Mexican riflemen. At this moment a bullet tore through his throat killing him instantly.

On September 22, Worth's Division in the west began its assault on the city's defenses. Twigg's Division, including the Baltimore Battalion, stood in reserve as the men under Worth charged and took the Bishop's Palace, a major Mexican army stronghold. Twigg's men found protection under an embankment as the Black Fort continued to bombard the infantry's positions to the north and east of the city. At dusk the unit returned to the woods San Domingo and camp.

The following day was more of the same: waiting, waiting, waiting.... Although Worth's Division continued its attack, Twigg's division stood in readiness for the entire day awaiting the order to move forward. The Baltimore Battalion again returned to camp at dusk, having sat out another day in the siege of Monterey.

Finally on Thursday, the 24th, victory came to the American forces. In the evening, the Baltimore Battalion was formed up to relieve the regulars holding the captured Fort Teneria. While on guard that evening, a messenger brought the word that General Taylor and General Ampudia had come to an agreement on the surrender of the city. Monterey had capitulated!

Following the surrender, the battalion maintained its camp outside of Monterey in the wood of San Domingo. On November 24, Major R.C. Buchanan, United States Army, became commander of the unit, replacing the gallant Watson. The unit buried the remaining dead from the battle and enjoyed this respite from the war. Effective December 10th, the battalion was transferred to a new organization, a Volunteer Brigade, commanded by General Quitman. Additional units joining the battalion were the 1st Mississippi, 1st Tennessee, and the 1st Georgia infantry regiments.

After nearly three months camped near Monterey, the Battalion began marching south on December 14, 1846. The move was welcomed by the troops as they departed for Victoria. While in camp on December 18th, the Volunteer Brigade was again reorganized into a division under the command of Brigadier General Quitman. One brigade was composed of the 1st and 2nd Tennessee regiments of foot, commanded by Colonel Campbell. The second brigade, commanded by Colonel Jackson, included the 1st Mississippi, 1st Georgia, and the Baltimore Battalion. The battalion reached Victoria on December 29th, via Linares, Villa Grande, and Hildago.

March South

In early January, 1847, Taylor's Army again was reorganized. By order of General Winfield Scott, Taylor's Army was to march north, while selected units were to join Scott's Army in Vera Cruz. On January 16th, the Baltimore Battalion was assigned to Quitman's Brigade of Patterson's Division consisting of the 1st Georgia and 4th Illinois Regiments, and a Tennessee Cavalry Company. The Brigade was to march to Tampico, sail to Vera Cruz and join Scott's forces from the United States. The Battalion arrived in Tampico on January 29th. By February 25th, the Baltimore Battalion joined other units in garrison duty at Tampico until the end of the unit's enlistment in May.

The Baltimore-Washington Battalion of Volunteers was officially mustered out on May 30, 1847. All men were provided with travel pay from Tampico to Baltimore or Washington City. Many of the volunteers complained that the government should provide transportation back to the United States, yet all of those willing to depart found ships destined for ports in the United States.

The Maryland and District of Columbia Regiment of Volunteers

In early June, a new regiment of volunteers was forming in Baltimore for the duration of the war. Lieutenant Colonel George Hughes was designated commander of the regiment to be called the District of Columbia (DC) and Maryland (MD) Regiment of Volunteers. Although primarily a Maryland regiment, during the course of the next year, three companies (Mounted Volunteers under Wheat, Infantry under Rowley, and Mounted Volunteers under Boyd) from Tennessee and Pennsylvania, were attached to the unit. The regiment was mustered into service at Fort McHenry and began transporting three companies aboard the transport ship *Alexandria* to Vera Cruz on July 23, 1847. The ship *Napier* carried an

War Department,
Adjutant General's Office,
Washington, Sept 30. 1847.

General Orders
  No 33.

By direction of the Secretary of War the "District of Columbia and Maryland Battalion of Volunteers" commanded by Lieutenant Colonel G. W. Hughes, will be organized into a regiment, under the Lieut Colonel, as Colonel, to be called the "District of Columbia and Maryland Regiment". The regiment will be composed of the four companies (including Captain Schaeffer's) raised in the District of Columbia; the four companies of Maryland Volunteers now in service; the company of Mounted Volunteers at Tampico commanded by Captain Joseph R. West; and Captain Chatham R. Wheat's company of Mounted Volunteers now serving with the army under Major General Scott. The two mounted companies will be considered as temporarily attached to the regiment, until two companies of infantry now being raised are completed.

By Order,
T. Thomas
Ast Adj Gen

General Order No. 33, establishing the District of Columbia and Maryland Regiment.

additional three companies. The *Alexandria* arrived at Vera Cruz on August 24th as the disembarking troops set up camp at Vergara, three miles from the city.

Five companies of the regiment, to include Captains Barry, Brown, Dolan, and Taylor, began their march west toward the unit's only major action for the remainder of the war. On September 6, 1847, the units left Vergara, marched through Sante Fe and across the river San Juan. The territory was covered by passes and hills that enabled small raiding bands of robbers and bandits to overwhelm their prey. The guerilla tactics used by these groups also took its toll on the marching columns of American troops.

The National Highway was a major route between Vera Cruz, Jalapa and Mexico City. The National Bridge, along that route, was a key element between the cities of Vera Cruz and Jalapa. In April, 1847, General Winfield Scott had taken the bridge and defeated Santa Anna's forces at the battle of Cerro Gordo. Unfortunately, General Scott was unable to leave a sufficient force to guard the passes along the highway. This resulted in the recapture of key transportation points along Scott's supply route by brigands and some regular Mexican forces.

On September 9th, the Maryland and District of Columbia Regiment reached the National Bridge. In the past few days, the regiment had been attacked several times by snipers and other small bands of men. On approach, a large fort was identified on the summit of a hill overlooking the bridge. The Mexicans had occupied the fort in an effort to guard the road and prevent further reinforcement of Scott's forces near Mexico City. The Maryland and District of Columbia Regiment accompanied by U.S. regulars broke into two columns flanking the road to the bridge. Artillery began firing at the fort in an effort to pin down the forces occupying the fort while the infantry companies attempted to flank the fort. A local guide, hired by the U.S. forces, agreed to show the Marylanders the access route to the rear of the fort. The access would afford surprise to the occupants of the fort; however, the approach was along a 50 feet high precipice with a vine providing the only means of ascent. First up the wall was Major Kenly and Captain Dolan's company of the regiment. In a short time three infantry companies and a dismounted dragoon company were in place ready for the assault. The continued firing of artillery had forced the Mexicans to remain hidden from view as the Marylanders began their charge. The Mexicans were taken entirely by surprise. Getting off only one round of fire, they escaped over the walls running north down the highway.

In early November, the regiment was ordered to Jalapa to perform garrison duty. The 13th U.S. Infantry Regiment relieved the MD and DC Volunteers on November 5th at the Natural Bridge. The regiment marched to Cedeno where it was brigaded with the 2nd Illinois and the Withers Rifle Battalion. In Jalapa, Lieutenant Colonel Hughes was appointed military governor in command of the regiment, the 2nd Illinois and a battalion of New Jersey volunteers. By December 4th, Tilghman's and Schaeffer's Companies arrived from the United States and, with two additional companies, joined the MD and DC Volunteer Regiment.

For the remainder of the war, the regiment continued on garrison duty at Jalapa. Occasionally, reports of bushwackers in the nearby passes summoned the unit to arms. During the next five months, several companies were called out to protect an incoming train passing through Cerro Gordo. The last major reorganization occurred in March with the unit coming under the divisional command of Major General Patterson.

Mexican General Santa Anna's capitulation of Mexico City and loss of the war resulted in his forced exile to Jamaica. While awaiting his final disposition, Santa Anna was retired to his hacienda in the Jalapa province in March, 1848. On March 30th, Captain Lloyd Tilghman of the Light Artillery Company was assigned the task of accompanying Santa Anna and his Mexican escort to the port of Vera Cruz for his departure from Mexico.[7] Tilghman and Lieutenant Tensfield with fifty men escorted the General through several Mexican towns and in one instance, tactfully avoided a skirmish with Mexican guerrillas in the town of Antiqua. Santa Anna embarked on the Spanish brig *Martine* on April 5th for Jamaica.

The War with Mexico ended on May 29, 1848. The regiment began preparations to return control of the government to local officials and move to Vera Cruz for return to the United States. By June 22nd, at least two companies had embarked on the steamer *James Day* destined for New Orleans and home.

Following the practice of earlier wars, an association of Mexican War veterans was established. As early as 1849, an association entitled "Maryland Volunteers in the Mexican War" was created. A committee on constitution and by-laws was active with George W. Talbott as chairman. The group appeared to be quite active throughout the 1850's. It is not certain whether this group merged with the larger organization called the "Association of Mexican War Veterans" which included veterans from other units and states, or whether it continued separately. However, by the mid-1880's, many of the Maryland members were also members of the larger group. It was this larger group which was instrumental in raising a monument to Watson and the Maryland volunteers in Baltimore during the early 1900's. As the veterans approached old age and memories of the War faded in the minds of the American Public so too did the vitality of the organization diminish. By the time the pensions terminated in 1926 the organization had disappeared from the local scene.

NOTES

1. J. Thomas Scharf, The Chronicles of Baltimore (Baltimore, 1874), p. 516.

2. Baltimore Sun, May 20, 1846, p. 2.

3. Peyton C. Nevitt, "Mexican War," in Washington--Past and Present, ed. John C. Proctor (New York, 1930), p. 374.

4. Allen Paine Mexican War Diary, MS-2674, Maryland Historical Society.

5. John Axer Letters, Mexican War Collection, MS-1902, Maryland Historical Society.

6. Although it would have been difficult to distinguish who were running since both regulars and volunteers were wearing the same uniform during this assault. It is generally assumed that volunteers would run before the regulars. However, considering the withering fire placed upon the attacking force, it is likely that the entire force broke and dashed for cover.

7. Tilghman, Lloyd Letter to Acting Military Governor of Jalapa.

COMPENDIUM OF MARYLAND AND DISTRICT OF COLUMBIA VOLUNTEERS

Information on the volunteers is given in the following order: Name - Rank - Unit - Place of enlistment - Age and date. For a complete explanation see page vii. (Note: All dates are in the following format: month/day/18__year, unless otherwise noted.)

Ackenback, John - G Company (Light Artillery)/Rgt., Baltimore, 28 (7/13/48).

Adams, John H., 4th Sergeant

Addison, Henry J., 1st Lieutenant - A Company/Rgt., Washington, 31 (7/24/48).

Aisquith, William E., Sergeant - E Company/Bn., Baltimore, Later promoted to Brevet 2nd Lieutenant and moved to adjutant in the battalion staff. Resident of Baltimore, he was the son of Captain Aisquith, who commanded a company of sharpshooters at the Battle of North Point in the War of 1812. Died on 6/29/56 in Washington City. (K-78) (H-671)

Albright, John S. 1st Corporal - A Company/Bn., Baltimore, 27 (5/30/47).

Alden, John, 3rd Sergeant - F Company/Bn., Baltimore, 28 (5/30/46).

Alden, John - H Company/Rgt., Baltimore, 33 (7/15/48).

Alderdice, John - F Company/Rgt., Baltimore, 18 (7/18/48). Wife, Sarah J., filed for pension on 10/3/88, number W-7211.

Alexander, John J., 3rd Sergeant - E Company/Rgt., Baltimore, 37 (7/18/48).

Alexander, John F. - E Company/Bn., Baltimore. Discharged by surgeon's certificate on (8/31/46) at Camargo. (K-69)

Alexander, William P. - A Company/Bn., Baltimore, 35 (10/2/46). Died of wounds received at Monterey.

Aley, John - A Company/Bn., Baltimore, 22 (5/30/47).

Allen, George - E Company/Bn., Baltimore, Slightly wounded at the Battle of Monterey on 9/21/46. (D-243)

Allen, James H. - F Company/Bn., Baltimore, 20 (5/30/46).

Allen, John E. - F Company/Bn., Baltimore, 22 (5/30/46).

Allen, John - E Company/Bn., Baltimore, 19 (12/31/46). Soldier filed for pension from residence in Indiana on 11/16/87, number S-17504. Received until death on 6/20/94. Wife, Amanda, also filed for pension, number W-12198.

COMPENDIUM OF VOLUNTEERS   13

Allen, William T. - E Company/Bn., Baltimore, 23 (12/31/46). Soldier filed for pension on 7/7/87, number S-14924.

Allender, Ellis J. - B Company/Bn., Baltimore. Soldier filed for pension from Virginia on 11/6/94, number S-24636.

Althouse, Tobias - B Company/Bn., Baltimore, 35 (5/30/46)

Anderman, Frederick - C Company/Rgt., Baltimore, 39. Died in the regimental hospital at Jalapa on 3/7/48.

Anderson, Aquilla - H Company/Rgt., Baltimore, 19 (7/15/48).

Anderson, Jesse - H Company/Rgt., Washington, 19 (7/15/48).

Anderson, John R. - B Company/Bn., Baltimore, 22 (5/30/46).

Anderson, John R. - H Company/Rgt., Baltimore, 22 (7/15/48).

Anderson, Thomas J. - F Company/Bn., Baltimore, 20 (5/30/46). Also served in Company F of the Regiment.

Andlum, John - C Company/Bn., Washington, 21 (2/28/47).

Andrews, John - E Company/Bn., Baltimore, 23 (12/31/46).

Appleby, Ridgely - D Company/Rgt., Washington, 21. Discharged by surgeon's certificate at Jalapa on 2/6/48.

Armacost, Joshua C. - B Company/Bn., Baltimore, 44 (5/30/46).

Armstrong, George - C Company/Rgt., Baltimore, 42 (4/30/48).

Armstrong, James - A Company/Bn., Baltimore, 20 (5/30/47). Also served in G Company (Light Artillery) of the Regiment.

Armstrong, Robert, 1st Corporal - C Company/Rgt., Baltimore, 19 (4/30/48).

Arthur, John - F Company/Rgt., Baltimore, 19. Discharged at Puente, Mexico on 9/24/47.

Atkinson, Lemuel - E Company/Bn., Baltimore, 23 (12/31/46).

Aunuld, George - B Company/Bn., Baltimore, Very severely wounded at the Battle of Monterey on 9/21/46. (D-243)

Axer, John, 2nd Sergeant - F Company/Bn., Baltimore, 28 (5/30/46).

Aydelott, Benjamin - F Company/Rgt., Baltimore, 19 (7/18/48).

Bacon, Joseph K. - D Company/Rgt., Philadelphia, 22. Discharged by surgeon's certificate from general hospital in Vera Cruz on 1/21/48.

Bailey, James - A Company/Rgt., Washington, 19 (7/24/48).

Baker, Charles F. - A Company/Rgt., Washington, 33 (7/24/48).

Baker, Henry J. - F Company/Rgt., Baltimore, 27 (7/18/48).

Baker, Jacob - E Company/Bn., Baltimore, 20 (12/31/46). Soldier filed for pension on 6/21/87, number S-14373.

Baker, John - B Company/Bn., Baltimore, 22 (5/30/46).

Baker, William H., 2nd Lieutenant - F Company/Rgt., Baltimore. Soldier filed for pension on 3/30/87, number S-7364.

Balderson, William S. - A Company/Bn., Baltimore, 21 (5/30/47). Wife, Sarah J., filed for pension from Wisconsin on 2/18/87, number W-88.

Ball, George - Recruit Company/Rgt., Baltimore, 19 (2/29/48). Alias George Tavenner. Soldier filed for pension on 3/17/87, number S-255. Soldier was residing at 915 S. Ann St, Baltimore in 1893. Ball also served in the U.S. Revenue Cutter Service aboard the ships, U.S.R.C. *Reliance* and *Tiger*. (L-3)

Ball, John - G Company (Light Artillery)/Rgt.

Ballman, John H., 2nd Lieutenant - A Company/Rgt., Washington, 33 (7/24/48). Wife, Marie, filed for pension from residence in the District of Columbia on 1/31/88, number W-5804.

Baney, William - E Company/Rgt., Baltimore, 37 (7/18/48). Sick in the hospital at Vera Cruz.

Bannister, William - E Company/Bn., Baltimore, 22 (12/31/46).

Barbour, Washington T. - D Company/Rgt., Washington, 18 (2/29/48).

Barclay, James - F Company/Rgt., Baltimore, 31. Discharged at Jalapa on 12/14/47.

Bares, John T. - G Company (Light Artillery)/Rgt., Baltimore, 28 (7/13/48). Died.

Barker, Samuel A., 2nd Corporal - H Company/Rgt., Baltimore, 21 (7/15/48).

Barker, Samuel P. - F Company/Bn., Baltimore, 20 (5/30/46).

Barnard, Fanning, Corporal - D Company/Bn., Washington. Soldier filed for pension from residence in District of Columbia on

7/29/87, number S-15481. Wife, Linda H., also filed under number W-19903.

Barnard, John H. - G Company (Light Artillery)/Rgt., Baltimore, 41 (7/13/48).

Barozy, Paul - H Company/Rgt., Jalapa, Mexico.

Barry, Daniel - D Company/Bn., Washington, 18 (2/28/47).

Barry, Edmund, Captain - B Company/Rgt., Washington, 28 (8/17/48). Wife, Juliana H., filed for pension from the District of Columbia on 3/14/87, number W-102.

Barthold, Christian - F Company/Rgt., Baltimore, 23 (7/18/48).

Bartman, Daniel - B Company/Bn., Baltimore, 18 (5/30/46).

Bartting, Thomas, 2nd Sergeant - F Company/Rgt., Baltimore, 35 (7/18/48).

Bauff, Henry - H Company/Rgt., Baltimore, 34. Died at the regimental hospital in 1848.

Bauff, John - H Company/Rgt., Washington. Died at the regimental hospital in 1848.

Baum, Louis - E Company/Rgt., Baltimore. Alias Ludwig Baum. Soldier filed for pension from Maryland on 3/14/89, number S-21356. Wife, Christina, filed for pension on 6/8/97, number W-13976.

Baxley, George C. - A Company/Bn., Baltimore, 41 (8/8/46). Discharged by surgeon's certificate at Camp Belknap.

Baxley, James - A Company/Bn., Baltimore, 23 (5/30/47). Soldier filed for pension on 2/4/87, number S-366. By 1895, James was blind. (L-3)

Beach, William - B Company/Rgt., Washington, 22. Discharged by surgeon's certificate at Jalapa on 3/15/48.

Beacham, James A., Corporal - E Company/Bn., Baltimore, 24 (12/31/46). Wife, Rosalba E., filed for pension from the District of Columbia on 3/4/98, number W-14436.

Beachum, Benjamin - B Company/Bn., Baltimore, 28 (5/30/46). Died from the effects of the heat in 7/46. (B-7/21/46-1)

Beale, William H. - H Company/Rgt., Washington, 21 (7/15/48).

Beall, John E. - B Company/Bn., Baltimore, 23 (5/30/46).

Beall, William H. - C Company/Bn., Washington, 30 (2/28/47). Soldier filed for pension on 6/7/87, number S-13963. Soldier was residing in Patapsco Neck, Baltimore County in 1895. (L-3)

Beam, J. Hileary - A Company/Rgt., Washington, 30's. Died in the general hospital at Vera Cruz on 11/12/47.

Bean, Josiah - B Company/Rgt., Washington, 24. Died at Camp Sardino in 1847.

Beaston, Samuel - E Company/Bn., Baltimore, 21 (12/31/46).

Beck, George - E Company/Rgt., Baltimore, 22 (7/18/48).

Beeler, Lewis F., 3rd Sergeant - C Company/Bn., Washington, 18 (2/28/47). Soldier filed for pension from Maryland on 12/20/90, number S-2324. Wife, Amanda, filed for pension on 6/3/1913, number W-20104. Mr. Beeler was born in Alexandria, Virginia and lived there until he was six. His family moved to Washington City, where he attended school until 1846. After residing in Baltimore for a short period, he moved his family to New York where he remained throughout the Civil War. Following the war, he returned to Baltimore and resided at 5 Broadway. There he was employed by the Baltimore and Ohio Railroad as yardmaster for Locust Point. In 1910 he had one son and two daughters living in Baltimore. (E-1910).

Bell, Phineas B., 1st Lieutenant - C Company/Bn., Washington.

Bell, Robert C., 2nd Lieutenant - C Company/Rgt., Baltimore.

Bell, William, 1st Sergeant - C Company/Rgt., Baltimore, 24 (4/30/48).

Bell, William - E Company/Rgt., Baltimore, 23 (7/18/48). Died on 1/8/87. Wife, Elizabeth J., filed for pension from Pennsylvania on 3/8/88, W-6047. Also see bounty land warrant 24141-160-47.

Belt, Richard H. - E Company/Bn., Baltimore. Drowned near Brazos Santiago on 7/3/46. He was a resident of Carroll County, Maryland. (K-38)

Bender, Jacob A., 3rd Corporal - A Company/Rgt., Washington, 26 (7/24/48).

Bennett, Davis - G Company (Light Artillery)/Rgt.

Bennett, George W. - F Company/Rgt., Baltimore, 22 (7/18/48).

Bennett, Lewis - G Company (Light Artillery)/Rgt., Baltimore, 28 (7/13/48).

Berger, Jacob, 3rd Corporal - C Company/Rgt., Baltimore, 28 (4/30/48).

Berry, Thomas - H Company/Rgt., Baltimore. Discharged on 10/4/47 at Fort McHenry.

Biddle, Richard - F Company/Rgt., Jalapa, Mexico.

Billington, Gover S. - A Company/Bn., Baltimore, 29 (9/46). Discharged by surgeon's certificate at Camargo. Later served in G Company (Light Artillery) of the Regiment.

Billington, John A. - E Company/Bn., Baltimore.

Birch, John D. - D Company/Rgt., Baltimore, 21 (2/29/48).

Blakenoy, Samuel - C Company/Rgt., Baltimore, 27 (4/30/48).

Blanchard, Constantine - B Company/Bn., Baltimore, 18 (5/30/46).

Boice, John M. - H Company/Rgt., Baltimore. Soldier filed for pension from Pennsylvania on 2/23/87, number S-580.

Bolkman, Frederick - G Company (Light Artillery)/Rgt., Baltimore, 19. Deserted from Fort McHenry on 9/1/47.

Bomberger, John H. - F Company/Rgt., Baltimore, 31 (7/18/48). Soldier filed for pension from Maryland on 2/4/87, number S-586. Wife, Rosa Ann, filed for pension on 6/2/96, W-13385.

Boss, Anthony - G Company (Light Artillery)/Rgt.

Boss, Isaac - G Company (Light Artillery)/Rgt., Baltimore, 18 (7/13/48).

Boswell, Thomas P. - H Company/Rgt., Baltimore, 22 (7/15/48).

Boswell, Thomas B., Corporal - D Company/Bn., Washington, 21 (2/28/47).

Boulanger, Edward - E Company/Bn., Baltimore. Discharged by surgeon's certificate on 8/7/46. (K-38)

Bowen, Alexander H., 3rd Sergeant - D Company/Rgt., Washington, 22 (2/29/48).

Bowers, George, 3rd Sergeant - C Company/Rgt., Baltimore, 26 (4/30/48).

Bowers, George - A Company/Bn., Baltimore, 20 (5/30/47).

Bowie, George W. - E Company/Bn., Baltimore, 34 (12/31/46).

Bowie, Oden, 2nd Lieutenant - E Company/Bn., Baltimore. Soldier filed for pension on 3/19/89, number S-21397. Bowie was born on November 10, 1826 in Prince George's County, Maryland. His parents were William D. Bowie and Eliza Oden, natives of the state. William served as state delegate to the House of Delegates for several terms and for six years in the State Senate. Eliza Oden Bowie died in 1835. Oden graduated from St. Mary's College, Baltimore in July, 1845. Subsequently he enlisted in the Baltimore Battalion in 1846 and was elevated to the rank of 2nd Lieutenant. Shortly after the Battle of Monterey, in which he participated, Bowie left the Battalion to become a senior captain in a U.S. Army regular regiment called the Voltigeurs. Illness forced Bowie to resign his commission and return to the United States. In 1847, he was elected to the House of Delegates and remained for several terms. In 1860 he served as the President of the Baltimore and Potomac Railroad. After winning the nomination as Democratic candidate in 1867, Bowie served as Governor of the State of Maryland between 1869 and 1873. Following his public service he became President of the Baltimore City Passenger Railway Company. His married Alice Carter. In 1879 all seven of their children were living. He died on 12/4/94 in Prince Georges County, Maryland; buried at the family cemetery in Fairview. (K-480) (O-670)

Bowman, Henry H. - H Company/Rgt., Baltimore. Solider filed for pension from Pennsylvania on 5/25/87, number S-15370.

Bowman, Joseph R. - B Company/Bn., Baltimore, 18 (5/30/46).

Boyd, James - F Company/Bn., Baltimore, 19 (5/30/46). Wife, Amelia M., filed for pension from Maryland on 1/5/1901, number W-15963.

Boyd, James, Captain - F Company/Bn., Baltimore. Later captain of an independent company attached to the regiment of volunteers. Killed in action at Rio Calaboso on 7/12/47. (H-672)

Boyd, John - E Company/Bn., Baltimore, 18 (12/31/46).

Boyd, William - F Company/Bn., Baltimore, 28 (12/31/46).

Boyer, William - F Company/Bn., Baltimore, 28 (12/31/46).

Boyle, Eugene, Captain - D Company/Bn., Washington, Promoted to Captain on 11/23/46, died at sea 1/6/47 while on leave of absence.

Boyle, Henry - G Company (Light Artillery)/Rgt.

Bradly, James, Musician - F Company/Rgt., Jalapa, Mexico.

Braley, Leonard H. - Wife, Annie C.C., filed for pension from the District of Columbia on 2/8/94, number W-11885.

Brand, Benjamin F., Corporal - E Company/Bn., Baltimore, 27 (12/31/46). Wounded near Monterey by a gang of Mexican desperadoes. (K-152)

Brandall, Joseph, 3rd Sergeant - H Company/Rgt., Baltimore, 33 (7/15/48).

Brannan, John, Sgt. Major - Regimental Staff, 32 (7/24/48).

Brazell, Malachi - Battalion. Wife, Nancy, filed for pension from Alabama on 2/29/88, number W-5990.

Brazier, John W. - E Company/Rgt., Baltimore, 20 (7/18/48).

Briceland, Benjamin - A Company/Bn., Baltimore, 28 (5/30/47).

Broadus, Edward - G Company (Light Artillery)/Rgt., Baltimore, 20. Deserted from Fort McHenry on 8/28/47.

Bromslea, Henry - C Company/Rgt., Baltimore, 40 (4/30/48).

Bronaugh, Robert, Captain - C Company/Bn., Washington.

Brooks, William H. - D Company/Rgt., Baltimore, 22. Discharged by surgeon's certificate at Jalapa on 2/6/48.

Brown, Addison - A Company/Rgt., Washington, 44 (7/24/48).

Brown, Allen - C Company/Bn., Washington, 33 (2/28/47).

Brown, Basil P. - F Company/Bn., Baltimore, 24 (5/30/46).

Brown, Bassel - H Company/Rgt., Baltimore. Died at the regimental hospital.

Brown, Charles P. - C Company/Bn., Washington, 37 (2/28/47).

Brown, George W., Captain - E Company/Rgt., Baltimore, 34 (7/18/48).

Brown, James - A Company/Bn., Baltimore, 25 (5/30/47). Soldier filed for pension from Maryland on 6/1/87, number S-7595. Wife, Margaret, filed for pension, number W-15625.

Brown, John, Musician - H Company/Rgt., Washington. Died in 1847.

Brown, John - A Company/Rgt., Baltimore, 25. Died in regimental hospital at Jalapa on 2/8/48.

Brown, Thomas - D Company/Bn., Washington, 22 (2/28/47).

Brown, William - F Company/Rgt., Baltimore, 21. Died at Jalapa on 4/19/48.

Bryerly, Wakeman, Asst. Surgeon of the Regiment.

20   MARYLAND AND D.C. VOLUNTEERS IN THE MEXICAN WAR

Buchanan, Robert C., Brevet Major, Commander of the Battalion Staff. Later a Brevet Major-General, U.S. Army, serving in the Peninsula campaign and the Battle of Antietam in the Civil War. Buchanan was a West Point graduate and career army soldier. He served between 7/1/30 until 1865, participating in the Blackhawk and Florida Wars as well as the Mexican and Civil War. A native Baltimorean and son of Andrew Buchanan, a merchant in the city, Buchanan maintained residence in Washington City. Died on 11/29/78. (K-479) (L-3) (Q-11/30/78-2)

Buckers, John - F Company/Rgt., Jalapa, Mexico.

Buckhaus, David - C Company/Rgt., Baltimore, 20 (4/30/48). Alias Louis Hamburger. Soldier filed for pension from Baltimore, Maryland on 1/12/88, number S-18170.

Buckley, James - G Company (Light Artillery)/Rgt.

Burnham, James H. - F Company/Rgt., Baltimore, 21 (7/18/48). Soldier filed for pension from Maryland on 3/30/87, number S-7658. Wife, Margaret, filed for pension on 7/13/1901, W-16292.

Burns, Benjamin F., 1st Sergeant - D Company/Rgt., Washington, 25 (2/29/48). Soldier filed for pension on 2/23/87, number S-891.

Burton, Abner - C Company/Bn., Washington, 24 (2/28/47).

Busey, James R. - F Company/Bn., Baltimore, 20 (5/30/46). Soldier filed for pension on 2/9/87, number S-914.

Bush, James William - B Company/Rgt., Washington, 22 (8/17/48).

Bush, William, Sr. - B Company/Rgt., Washington, 42. Discharged by surgeon's certificate at Jalapa on 3/15/48.

Butler, David - B Company/Rgt., Washington, 39 (8/17/48).

Butler, David - F Company/Rgt., Jalapa, Mexico.

Butler, George W. - A Company/Bn., Baltimore, 22 (5/30/47).

Butler, William A. - E Company/Bn., Baltimore, 18 (12/31/46). Wife, Mary A., filed for pension from Maryland on 7/27/87, number W-4314.

Byram, Edward I. - E Company/Bn., Baltimore.

Byrne, Thomas - A Company/Bn., Baltimore, 22 (8/8/46). Discharged by surgeon's certificate at Camp Belknap.

Cameron, William H. - Wife, Susan, filed for pension on 3/3/91, number W-9693.

COMPENDIUM OF VOLUNTEERS 21

Camper, Frances - E Company/Rgt., Baltimore, 20 (7/18/48).

Camsten, Joseph - E Company/Rgt., Baltimore, 25 (7/18/48).

Canning, James B. - E Company/Bn., Baltimore. Discharged by surgeon's certificate on (8/31/46) at Camargo. (K-69)

Caples, Robert - A Company/Bn., Baltimore, Very dangerously wounded at the Battle of Monterey on 9/21/46. (D-243)

Carr, John, 2nd Lieutenant - B Company/Rgt., Washington, 24 (8/17/48).

Carr, William M., 2nd Sergeant - A Company/Bn., Baltimore, 22 (4/30/48). Promoted to sergeant and transferred. Also served in C Company of the Regiment as a 2nd Sergeant.

Carraw, James - G Company (Light Artillery)/Rgt., Baltimore, 21 (7/13/48).

Carroll, John W. - A Company/Bn., Baltimore, 26 (9/46). Discharged by surgeon's certificate at Camargo.

Carroll, William - C Company/Bn., Washington, 23 (2/28/47). Also served in A Company of the Regiment.

Cassles, Robert M. - A Company/Bn., Baltimore, 19 (10/27/46). Died of wounds received at Monterey.

Caster, Joseph - E Company/Rgt., Baltimore, 20 (7/18/48).

Caster, Thomas - E Company/Rgt., Baltimore, 22 (7/18/48).

Castleman, Nathaniel G. - H Company/Rgt., Baltimore. Discharged at Fort McHenry on 10/9/47 due to age (minor).

Chambers, Benjamin F. - G Company (Light Artillery)/Rgt., Baltimore, 19 (7/13/48).

Chambers, John Thomas, 1st Sergeant - E Company/Rgt., Baltimore, 20 (7/18/48).

Chapman, David T., Brevet 2nd Lieutenant - A Company/Bn., Baltimore.

Childs, George A. - A Company/Bn., Baltimore, 20 (8/12/46). Died of fever at Camp Belknap.

Chipps, David - C Company/Bn., Washington, 22 (2/28/47).

Chorman, Ernest G., Sergeant - B Company/Bn., Baltimore, 18 (5/30/46). Soldier filed for pension on 4/1/1900, number S-25178.

Christopher, Arthur John - G Company (Light Artillery)/Rgt., Baltimore, 18 (7/13/48). Wife, Christina A.E., filed for pension from Maryland on 6/28/87, number W-3941.

Clark, George - E Company/Rgt., Baltimore, 19 (7/18/48).

Clark, John - E Company/Rgt., Baltimore, 32 (7/18/48).

Clark, John A. - E Company/Rgt., Baltimore, 41 (7/18/48). Sick in Baltimore.

Clark, Robert - A Company/Rgt., Baltimore, 33 (7/24/48).

Clark, Samuel T. - B Company/Rgt., Washington, 19 (8/17/48). Soldier filed for pension on 2/14/87, number S-1162.

Clark, William - E Company/Rgt., Baltimore, 27 (7/18/48).

Clarke, Joshua C. - B Company/Bn., Baltimore, 19 (5/30/46). Soldier filed for pension from the District of Columbia on 2/4/87, number S-1154. Wife, Ann M., filed for pension on 7/6/1901, number W-16280.

Clarke, Marcellus - D Company/Rgt., Washington, 19 (2/29/48). Soldier filed for pension from West Virginia on 4/11/90, number S-22643. Wife, Lucy F., filed for pension on 5/18/1903, number W-17112.

Claypool, William, Sergeant - A Company/Bn., Baltimore, 32 (5/30/47).

Clayrole, William - A Company/Bn., Baltimore.

Cleary, James - Recruit Company/Rgt., Baltimore, 28 (2/29/48). Soldier filed for pension on 2/12/87, number S-25499.

Cleggett, Otho - Recruit Company/Rgt., Baltimore, 30 (4/30/48).

Clements, James - G Company (Light Artillery)/Rgt., Baltimore, 19 (7/13/48).

Clemmens, Christopher C. - D Company/Rgt., Washington, 19 (2/29/48).

Clemments, Dominick - B Company/Rgt., Washington, 22 (8/17/48). Soldier filed for pension on 3/8/87, number S-1174.

Clifford, William - F Company/Rgt., Baltimore, 20 (7/18/48).

Cline, George - G Company (Light Artillery)/Rgt., Baltimore, 31 (7/13/48).

Cloomy, John - B Company/Bn., Baltimore, 25 (5/30/46).

Coady, Francis - C Company/Bn., Washington, 31 (2/28/47).

COMPENDIUM OF VOLUNTEERS   23

Transferred to company D on 1/16/47.

Cochran, James R. - D Company/Bn., Washington, 19 (2/28/47). Also served in H Company of the Regiment. Soldier filed for pension 8/25/88, number S-20160.

Cockran, Patrick - E Company/Rgt., Baltimore, 19 (7/18/48).

Coe, Robert - A Company/Rgt., Washington, 26 (7/24/48). Soldier filed for pension on 2/25/87, number S-1209.

Colb, Frederick - A Company/Rgt., Washington, 35. Died in the regimental hospital at Jalapa on 2/16/48.

Cole, Frances - E Company/Rgt., Baltimore.

Cole, George W. - A Company/Bn., Baltimore, 19 (7/4/46). Died of fever on-board the Transport Massachusetts enroute to Mexico.

Collins, George - F Company/Rgt., Baltimore, 27 (7/18/48). Wife, Caroline, filed for pension from Maryland on 10/18/87, number W-5722.

Collins, George N. - E Company/Bn., Baltimore, 30 (12/31/46).

Cologan, Thomas - B Company/Bn., Baltimore, 21 (5/30/46).

Connelly, James - E Company/Rgt., Baltimore, 20 (7/18/48). Soldier filed for pension on 8/3/87, number S-15628.

Connelly, James - B Company/Rgt., Washington, 36. Discharged by surgeon's certificate at Vera Cruz on 2/24/48.

Connolly, Edward - H Company/Rgt., Baltimore, 30 (7/15/48).

Cook, Mason G. - D Company/Rgt., Washington, 26 (2/29/48).

Cook, Robert, Corporal - G Company (Light Artillery)/Rgt., Baltimore, 21. Deserted from Fort McHenry on 8/26/47. Discharged by surgeon's certificate from Fort McHenry on 3/22/48.

Cook, William - H Company/Rgt., Baltimore, 36 (7/15/48).

Cook, William B. - G Company (Light Artillery)/Rgt., Baltimore, 32 (7/13/48). Deserted.

Cooley, Edward J. - G Company (Light Artillery)/Rgt., Baltimore, 22 (7/13/48). Soldier filed for pension from Maryland on 3/31/87, number S-7894. Wife, name unknown, also applied for pension on 2/17/1906, number W-18319. Soldier resided on Stricker Street, Baltimore in 1880. (L-4)

Cooper, James A. - D Company/Bn., Washington, 25 (2/28/47).

Cooper, John H. - B Company/Bn., Baltimore, 20 (5/30/46).

Cooper, John W. - Recruit Company. Soldier filed for pension on 9/12/89, number S-22057.

Cootes, George A. - Wife, Ellen, filed for pension on 5/20/92, number W-10648.

Copperstone, John - B Company/Bn., Baltimore, 27 (5/30/46).

Corbell, William G. - Wife, Louisa, filed for pension from Pennsylvania on 3/15/87, number W-408.

Corcoran, William J., 1st Lieutenant - H Company/Rgt., Baltimore.

Corey, Michael F. - F Company/Rgt., Baltimore, 21 (7/18/48). Wife, Rebecca W., filed for pension from Maryland on 4/27/87, number W-2788.

Cornwell, Benson - A Company/Rgt., Washington, 40 (7/24/48).

Costello, Henry R. - B Company/Bn., Baltimore, 27 (5/30/46).

Coster, Joseph - Wife, Ellen, filed for pension from Maryland on 3/12/87, number W-411. Died prior to 1879. (L-4)

Coster, Thomas H. - Wife, Annie E., filed for pension from Maryland on 8/24/1901, number W-16347. Died prior to 1879. (L-4)

Coupland, William G. - F Company/Bn., Baltimore, 19 (5/30/46).

Cover, Daniel - D Company/Bn., Washington, 20 (2/28/47).

Cowen, Thomas - B Company/Rgt., Baltimore, 19 (8/17/48).

Craddock, William H. - F Company/Bn., Baltimore, 21 (5/30/46).

Craft, Edward B. - C Company/?. Soldier filed for pension on 2/4/87, number S-3763.

Craig, Joshua - A Company/?. Soldier filed for pension on 2/26/87, number S-1452.

Creamer, John, Corporal - E Company/Bn., Baltimore, 28 (12/31/46). Wife, Cornelia, filed for pension from Maryland on 4/7/87, number W-444.

Cresman, Michael - B Company/Rgt., Baltimore, 32. Died at Vera Cruz on 1228/47.

Cripps, John F. - H Company/Rgt., Baltimore, 18 (7/15/48).

Crone, Robert H. - Recruit Company/Rgt., Baltimore, 20 (4/30/48).

COMPENDIUM OF VOLUNTEERS 25

Crone, William C. - Recruit Company/Rgt., Baltimore, 19 (4/30/48). Soldier filed for pension from Maryland on 2/4/87, number S-1479. Wife, Sarah A., filed for pension on 3/15/87, number W-447.

Cross, Thomas - D Company/Bn., Washington, 28 (2/28/47). Soldier filed for pension on 2/5/87, number S-1487.

Crough, John S. - F Company/Bn., Baltimore, 20 (5/30/46). Soldier filed for pension on 2/4/87, number S-1484.

Crown, Francis J. - G Company (Light Artillery)/Rgt., Baltimore, 21. Deserted from Fort McHenry on 8/25/47.

Cunin, Samuel - Recruit Company/Rgt., Baltimore, 37 (4/30/48).

Currier, Samuel - B Company/Bn., Baltimore, 34 (5/30/46). Later rejoined regiment and was in the recruit company on 2/29/48.

Curry, David - A Company/Rgt., Baltimore, 34. Sick at Vera Cruz 9/6/47 to 7/24/48.

Cutting, DeAzro A.B. - E Company/Bn., Baltimore. Discharged by surgeon's certificate on 8/7/46. (K-38)

Darley, John W. - D Company/Bn., Washington, 23 (2/28/47).

Darley, Thomas A. - Recruit Company/Rgt., Baltimore, 31 (2/29/48).

Daughady, Richard - G Company (Light Artillery)/Rgt., Baltimore, 36 (7/13/48).

Dawes, Josephus, 2nd Sergeant - C Company/Bn., Washington, 22 (2/28/47)

Davis, Ludwell H., 4th Corporal - H Company/Rgt., Washington, 24 (7/15/48). Promoted to Corporal on 5/2/48.

Day, Alfred, Sgt. Major in the Battalion Staff.

Day, Alfred - B Company/Bn., Baltimore, 22 (5/30/46).

Day, John, Corporal - B Company/Rgt., Washington, 37 (8/17/48).

Day, Samuel - G Company (Light Artillery)/Rgt., Baltimore, 35 (7/13/48).

De Corsey, Thomas - F Company/Rgt., Baltimore, 18 (2/29/48). Wife, Johanna, filed for pension from Maryland on 3/15/87, number W-503.

Deakins, John - A Company/Rgt., Washington, 40 (7/24/48).

Deckard, Jacob C. - C Company/Rgt., Baltimore, 25 (4/30/48).

26   MARYLAND AND D.C. VOLUNTEERS IN THE MEXICAN WAR

Deckard, John - C Company/Rgt., Baltimore, 20 (4/30/48).

Degant, Joseph - A Company/Bn., Baltimore, 21 (5/30/47).

Degges, William H., Captain, Commanding Officer - A Company/Rgt., Washington, 35 (7/24/48).

Degomp, Jacob - E Company/Bn., Baltimore, 20 (4/30/48). Also served in C Company of the Regiment. Discharged by surgeon's certificate on (8/31/46) at Camargo. (K-69)

Dement, William E. - C Company/Bn., Washington, 19 (2/28/47). Soldier filed for pension on 3/29/89, number S-21446. Soldier residing on the corner of Charles and Conway Streets in 1887. (L-5)

Demmitt, Joshua - Recruit Company/Rgt., Baltimore, 24 (2/29/48). Deserted from Fort McHenry on 3/15/48, apprehended on 3/20/48.

Dermidy, Walter - H Company/Rgt., Baltimore, 27 (7/15/48).

Derr, John - B Company/Rgt., Baltimore, 34. Died at Camp Sardino on 11/12/47.

Develin, William H. - Recruit Company/Rgt., Baltimore, 32 (2/29/48).

Devyer, Thomas - B Company/Bn., Baltimore, 39 (5/30/46).

Dick, Joseph H. - E Company/Bn., Baltimore, 22 (12/31/46). Soldier filed for pension on 7/9/87, number S-1744.

Dick, Peter - C Company/Bn., Washington, 29 (2/28/47).

Dickson, George P. - F Company/Bn., Baltimore, 19 (5/30/46).

Dimmitt, Joshua - B Company/Bn., Baltimore, 22 (5/30/46).

Dise, John - E Company/Rgt., Baltimore, 27 (7/18/48).

Dobbin, Francis M. - E Company/Bn., Baltimore.

Dobbin, William, Corporal - C Company/Bn., Washington, 21 (2/28/47). Died on 5/22/1910 in Rohnerville, California. Soldier filed for pension from California on 10/19/87, number S-17069. Wife, Ellen, filed for pension on 6/28/1910. Also see bounty land warrant 5412-160-47.

Dolan, Lawrence, 2nd Lieutenant - B Company/Bn., Baltimore, Later promoted to Captain and commanding officer of C Company of the Regiment. On sick furlough from 3/1/48 to 4/30/48.

Dolan, William - B Company/Rgt., Baltimore, 26 (8/17/48).

Dolson, Vernon, Corporal - B Company/Rgt., Washington, 18 (8/17/48).

Donally, John - C Company/Bn., Washington, 22 (2/28/47).

Donavan, Jeremiah H. - B Company/Bn., Baltimore, 18 (5/30/46).

Donnelly, John - Recruit Company/Rgt., Baltimore, 21. Deserted from Fort McHenry on 7/19/47.

Donnely, Robert S. - A Company/Bn., Baltimore, 20 (5/30/47). Wife, Marcellena, filed for pension from Colorado on 5/13/96, number W-13346.

Dorsey, Francis, Musician - B Company/Rgt., Baltimore, 9 (8/17/48).

Dorsey, Francis, Jr. - B Company/Rgt., Washington, 35. Discharged by surgeon's certificate at Vera Cruz on 2/5/48. Soldier filed for pension on 7/15/87, number S-15141.

Dove, George M., Dr., Surgeon - Battalion Staff, Departed with the sick for the United States on 8/7/46. He was a resident of Washington City. (K-38). Wife, Sarah A., filed for pension from the District of Columbia on 1/14/87, number W-5547.

Dowden, Raymond P., 2nd Lieutenant - A Company/Rgt., Washington, 32. Discharged from service on 1/19/48.

Downy, Hugh - B Company/Rgt., Washington, 19. Discharged by surgeon's certificate at Fort McHenry on 7/17/47.

Doyle, Samuel B., Sergeant - F Company/Rgt., Baltimore, 19. Discharged at Jalapa on 2/8/48. Soldier filed for pension from Maryland on 5/23/88, number S-19460. Wife, Rosalie C., filed for pension on 7/18/93, number 11493.

Drudge, George - B Company/Rgt., Washington, 23 (8/17/48).

Drudge, William - B Company/Rgt., Washington, 22 (8/17/48). Soldier filed for pension on 4/27/87, number S-11566.

Dudley, William - Wife, Mary F., filed for pension on 8/9/87, number W-4429.

Dulaney, William S. - D Company/Bn., Washington, 20 (2/28/47). Alias Lewis, William. Wife, Mary A. Lewis, filed for pension from Maryland on 5/2/87, number W-2834.

Duncan, Louis, Corporal - F Company/Bn., Baltimore, 20 (5/30/46).

Duncan, Thomas - B Company/Rgt., Washington, 20 (8/17/48).

Dungan, Alexander - F Company/Rgt., Baltimore, 40. Died at Jalapa in 1/48.

MARYLAND AND D.C. VOLUNTEERS IN THE MEXICAN WAR

Dungan, Henry - C Company/Bn., Washington, 20 (2/28/47).

Duval, Edward J. - D Company/Bn. Alias John C. Johnston. Soldier filed for pension from Pennsylvania on 11/3/90, number S-23170.

Dwyer, Thomas - D Company/Bn., Washington, 20 (2/28/47). Soldier filed for pension from Maryland on 6/27/87, number S-14614. Wife, Margaret A., filed for pension on 1/8/1907, number W-18580.

Eahe, Henry - A Company/Rgt., Washington, 31 (7/24/48).

Edmonson, Nathan - H Company/Rgt., Baltimore, (7/15/48). Discharged by surgeon's certificate at Jalapa on 3/15/48.

Edwards, John J. - A Company/Bn., Baltimore, 34 (5/30/47).

Edwards, Joseph - F Company/Rgt., Baltimore, 20. Discharged at Jalapa on 1/1/48.

Edwards, Thomas W. - H Company/Rgt., Washington, 37 (7/15/48). Sick in the hospital at Pittsburg, Pennsylvania. Wife, Jane F., filed for pension from Maryland on 2/8/87, number W-599.

Egan, John Thomas - E Company/Rgt., Baltimore. Discharged by surgeon's certificate at Jalapa on 2/6/48.

Ehrman, Charles H., 4th Sergeant - F Company/Bn., Baltimore, 25 (5/30/46). Later served as 4th Sergeant in F Company of the Regiment. Soldier filed for pension on 3/7/87, number S-1964.

Eld, Henry - C Company/Bn., Washington, 22 (2/28/47).

Elflin, George - A Company/Rgt., Washington, 30 (7/24/48).

Elliott, James - B Company/Bn., Baltimore, 30 (5/30/46).

Ellis, William H. - F Company/?. Wife, Elizabeth J., filed for pension from Maryland on 3/26/94, number W-11978.

Elting, Henry J. - E Company/Bn., Baltimore, 28 (12/31/46). Slightly wounded at the Battle of Monterey on 9/21/46. (D-243)

Emory, Lewis - C Company/Bn., Washington, 27 (1/14/47). Discharged by surgeon's certificate at Monterey.

Emory, William H., Lt. Colonel, Deputy commander of the Regiment. Officer in the Topographical Engineers, joined regiment on 4/23/48. During the Civil War, he served as a Brevet Major-General commanding the 19th Army Corps in Louisiana and Texas and later the Army of Virginia. (K-431) (K-482)

Epsedine, James - H Company/Rgt., Washington, 27 (7/15/48). Wife, Margaret, filed for pension from Pennsylvania on 5/1/90, number W-8951.

Eslinger, Christian - B Company/Rgt., Baltimore, 44. Discharged by surgeon's certificate at Vera Cruz on 2/5/48.

Fagan, Cornelius - H Company/Rgt., Baltimore, 19 (7/15/48).

Faherty, Joseph - B Company/Bn., Baltimore, 25 (5/30/46).

Fairall, Alfred - H Company/Rgt., Baltimore, 19 (7/15/48).

Falbush, Henry - Battalion, Reported to be sick at San Luis, Mexico on 5/24/47. (B-5/24/47-1)

Fasnaught, George - D Company/Bn., Washington, 21 (2/28/47).

Fay, William - A Company/Bn., Baltimore, 28 (5/30/47).

Fergi, J. - B Company/Rgt., Baltimore, 22 (8/17/48).

Ferney, John S. - A Company/Bn., Baltimore, 22 (5/30/47).

Files, Joseph - A Company/Bn., Baltimore, 24 (10/1/46). Discharged by surgeon's certificate due to wounds received at Monterey. Wife filed for pension from Maryland on 3/15/87, number W-655. Died on 12/2/79. (L-7)

Finlay, John J. - F Company/Bn., Baltimore, 19 (5/30/46). Soldier filed for pension on 2/9/87, number S-2194.

Finlay, William H. - G Company (Light Artillery)/Rgt., Baltimore, 33 (7/13/48).

Finnegan, Peter - A Company/Rgt., Baltimore, 30's. Died in quarters at camp in Mexico on 11/27/47.

Finnegan, Phillip - D Company/Rgt., Washington, 32 (2/29/48).

Fischer, Charles - E Company/Bn., Baltimore, 21 (12/31/46).

Fish, John - E Company/Rgt., Baltimore. Discharged by surgeon's certificate at Jalapa on 2/6/48.

Fisher, Francis - E Company/Bn., Baltimore. Discharged by surgeon's certificate on (8/31/46) at Camargo. (K-69)

Fisher, Henry - A Company/Rgt., Washington, 31 (7/24/48).

Fisher, John T. - H Company/Rgt., Baltimore, 23 (7/15/48).

Fitch, H.S., 1st Sergeant - C Company/Bn., Washington, 43 (2/28/47)

MARYLAND AND D.C. VOLUNTEERS IN THE MEXICAN WAR

Fitzgerald, Thomas, Corporal - D Company/Bn., Washington, 19 (2/28/47).

Fitzpatrick, Owen - F Company/Bn., Baltimore, 20 (5/30/46). Wife, Mary, filed for pension from Maryland on 6/1/91, number W-9908.

Fitzsimmons, John - E Company/Rgt., Baltimore, 24. Deserted from Fort McHenry in July, 1847.

Fleurix, James M. - F Company/Bn., Baltimore, 21 (5/30/46).

Flood, William - E Company/Rgt., Baltimore, 22 (7/18/48).

Floyd, Albion H.P. - D Company/Rgt., Baltimore, 24 (2/29/48).

Flynn, Thomas - A Company/Bn., Baltimore, 21 (5/30/47).

Forbes, William - H Company/Rgt. Soldier filed for pension from Ohio on 9/30/87, number S-16813. Wife, Mary E., filed for pension on 11/27/88, number W-7414.

Forbush, Henry - E Company/Bn., Baltimore, 22 (12/31/46). Killed on 1/23/47 near Tampico, Mexico by Mexican Lancers. (K-219)

Fordenburg, John - E Company/Rgt., Baltimore, 30 (7/18/48). Sick in hospital at Fort McHenry.

Fornshill, James - E Company/Rgt., Baltimore, 24 (7/18/48).

Forrest, David C., 4th Sergeant - D Company/Rgt., Washington, 19 (2/29/48). Wife, Catherine S., filed for pension from the District of Columbia on 5/14/87 (no number given).

Forsyth, William A. - G Company (Light Artillery)/Rgt., Baltimore, 20 (7/13/48). Discharged by civil process on 4/11/48.

Foster, William - E Company/Rgt., Baltimore, 33 (7/18/48).

Foust, John, Artificer - G Company (Light Artillery)/Rgt., Baltimore, 24 (7/13/48). Soldier filed for pension on 4/8/87, number S-8277.

Fowler, Jesse - B Company/Rgt., Washington, 30. Discharged by surgeon's certificate at Vera Cruz on 7/48.

Frank, Frederick, Musician - C Company/Rgt., Baltimore, 33 (4/30/48).

Frazier, W.L., Surgeon - C Company/Bn., Washington. (N-5/20/46-1)

Freeburger, George A., Sergeant - A Company/Bn., Baltimore, 24 (5/30/47). Soldier filed for pension from Maryland on 3/11/87, number S-2328. Wife, Theresa, filed for pension in 4/13/1909, number W-19293. Soldier resided at 521 Scott Street, Baltimore in 1895. (L-7)

Freed, George K. - G Company (Light Artillery)/Rgt.

Frost, James - A Company/Bn., Baltimore, 27 (5/30/47).

Fuller, Louis - E Company/Bn., Baltimore, 22 (12/31/46).

Fultz, George S., Corporal - C Company/Bn., Washington, 30 (2/28/47).

Fury, John G. - C Company/Rgt., Baltimore, 21 (4/30/48). Soldier resided at 9 Penn St., Baltimore in 1895. (L-7)

Gad, Owen, Sergeant - B Company/Bn., Baltimore.

Gaddess, Alexander Jr. - F Company/Bn., Baltimore, 20 (5/30/46).

Gallager, William - B Company/Bn., Baltimore, 18 (5/30/46).

Gallighan, William J. - Recruit Company/Rgt., Baltimore, 27. Discharged by surgeon's certificate from Fort McHenry on 3/26/48.

Galloway, John T.A., Drummer - E Company/Rgt., Baltimore, 18 (7/18/48). Soldier filed for pension on 7/26/87, number S-15409. Soldier resided at 1628 N. Wolf St., Baltimore in 1895. (L-8)

Gammill, Thomas - B Company/Rgt., Washington, 30 (8/17/48).

Gardiner, John - B Company/Bn., Baltimore, 30 (5/30/46).

Gardner, George T. - B Company/Rgt., Washington, 33. Died at Jalapa on 2/28/48.

Gardner, James F. - F Company/Bn., Baltimore, 20 (5/30/46).

Gardner, John - F Company/Bn., Baltimore, 28 (5/30/46).

Garretson, David - B Company/Bn., Baltimore, 18 (5/30/46).

Garrison, Bartlett - A Company/Rgt., Washington, 20's. Died in general hospital at Vera Cruz on 9/22/47.

Garrison, Joseph - A Company/Bn., Baltimore, 18 (9/46). Discharged by surgeon's certificate at Camargo.

Gary, William J. - Regiment. Soldier filed for pension on 2/2/87, number S-2437.

Gassaway, James Madison, 3rd Sergeant - D Company/Bn., Washington, 33 (2/28/47). Wife, Lucinda, filed for pension from the District of Columbia on 2/18/87, number W-747.

32   MARYLAND AND D.C. VOLUNTEERS IN THE MEXICAN WAR

Gates, William J. - A Company/Rgt., Washington, 22 (7/24/48).

Gaule, Patrick - E Company/Rgt., Baltimore, 23 (7/18/48).

Gayhart, Joseph - H Company/Rgt., Baltimore, 26 (7/15/48).

Geary, William J., 2nd Lieutenant - B Company/Rgt., Washington, 24 (8/17/48).

Gelston, Samuel - E Company/Bn., Baltimore, 23 (12/31/46).

Genty, Antonia - C Company/Bn., Washington, 34 (2/28/47).

Gerborth, Christian - C Company/Rgt., Baltimore, 45 (4/30/48).

Gerhardt, J.C.F. - G Company (Light Artillery)/Rgt., Baltimore, 23. Deserted from Fort McHenry on 9/2/47.

Gerney, John G. - A Company/Bn.

Geweke, Earnest - E Company/Rgt., Baltimore, 29 (7/18/48).

Gibson, George T. - B Company/Rgt., Washington, 39 (8/17/48).

Gibson, William - B Company/Bn., Baltimore, 22 (5/30/46). Soldier filed for pension on 3/7/87, number S-2479.

Gibson, William H. - C Company/Bn., Washington, 19 (2/28/47). Wife, Martha A., filed for pension from the District of Columbia on 3/3/87, number W-756.

Gier, Christian - A Company/Rgt., Washington, 30 (7/24/48).

Gife, Edward - D Company/Rgt., Baltimore, 44 (2/29/48).

Giffen, Robert - A Company/Bn., Baltimore, 22 (5/30/47). Alias William Steele. Soldier filed for pension from Texas on 4/5/87, S-10328.

Gifford, Henry - F Company/Bn., Baltimore, 27 (12/12/46). Discharged by surgeon's certificate at Monterey. Slightly wounded at the Battle of Monterey on 9/21/46. (D-243)

Gill, Edward - G Company (Light Artillery)/Rgt., Baltimore, 20 (7/13/48).

Gill, Edward - D Company/Rgt., Baltimore, 44 (2/29/48).

Gillingham, Horace H. - F Company/Bn., Baltimore, 24 (5/30/46). Deserted.

Gitner, Philip - A Company/Rgt., Baltimore, 36 Sick at general hospital in New Orleans 7/2/48 to 7/24/48.

Glass, Thomas - F Company/Bn., Baltimore, 19 (5/30/46).

Gleason, Thomas M., 1st Lieutenant - C Company/Bn., Washington. Died on 7/16/48. (H-672)

Glover, Edward R., Sergeant - B Company/Rgt., Washington, 24. Died at Jalapa on 12/11/47.

Glover, John W., 1st Sergeant - A Company/Rgt., Washington, 26 (7/24/48).

Goaphu, George - A Company/Rgt., Baltimore, 23 Sick at Vera Cruz 11/6/47 to 7/24/48.

Goddard, Calvin - D Company/Bn., Washington, 24 (2/28/47).

Goddard, Calvin - H Company/Rgt., Washington, 26 (7/15/48).

Goerl, Samuel - E Company/Rgt., Baltimore, 23 (7/18/48).

Goodrich, Thomas J. - G Company (Light Artillery)/Rgt., Baltimore, 18 (7/13/48).

Gordon, George - E Company/Bn., Baltimore. Discharged by surgeon's certificate on (8/31/46) at Camargo. (K-69)

Gordon, Josias B., 4th Corporal - E Company/Rgt., Baltimore, 39 (7/18/48).

Gordon, Nathaniel - H Company/Rgt., Baltimore. Discharged due to civil process at Fort McHenry on 10/6/47.

Gorman, James - D Company/Rgt., Washington, 38 (2/29/48).

Gorman, Patrick - F Company/Rgt., Baltimore, 19 (7/18/48).

Gorman, William, Corporal - D Company/Rgt., Baltimore, 19 (2/29/48).

Gosnell, Enoch - A Company/Bn., Baltimore, 22 (5/30/47).

Gosnell, Joshua - A Company/Bn., Baltimore, 24 (5/30/47).

Gould, Charles W. - A Company/Bn., Baltimore, 21 (1/14/47) Discharged on surgeon's certificate for a disability at Monterey on 1/14/47.

Graham, James - F Company/Rgt., Baltimore, 24 (7/18/48).

Graham, John - G Company (Light Artillery)/Rgt., Baltimore, 18 (7/13/48). Discharged by civil process.

Gray, Benjamin F. - A Company/Bn., Baltimore, 23 (5/30/47).

Gray, John T. - A Company/Bn., Baltimore, 19 (5/30/47). Became a court clerk in Baltimore City and resided at Broadway and Milliman Streets, Baltimore in 1895. Died on 11/13/95. (L-8)

Gray, Walter B. - A Company/Bn., Baltimore, 26 (9/46). Discharged by surgeon's certificate at Camargo.

Green, Daniel - F Company/Rgt., Jalapa, Mexico, 20 (7/18/48).

Green, Noah - H Company/Rgt., Baltimore, 25 (7/15/48).

Greene, George G. - F Company/Bn., Baltimore, 20 (5/30/46).

Greenwood, Charles H. - F Company/Rgt., Baltimore, 27 (7/18/48).

Gregory, James - G Company (Light Artillery)/Rgt.

Grey, Anthony - B Company/Rgt., Washington, 20 (8/17/48).

Grey, Nathaniel - B Company/Rgt., Washington, 30. Discharged by surgeon's certificate at Jalapa on 3/15/48.

Griffith, David A., 2nd Lieutenant - H Company/Rgt., Baltimore. Applied for pension from Pennsylvania on 9/19/88, number S-20339.

Griffith, Edward - H Company/Rgt., Baltimore, 19 (7/15/48).

Grimes, John - B Company/Rgt., Washington, 26. Died at Jalapa on 4/2/48.

Gronewell, John H.. 2nd Lieutenant - E Company/Rgt., Baltimore, 26 (7/18/48).

Grumble, James - H Company/Rgt., Baltimore. Died at the regimental hospital in 1848.

Gun, Thomas F. - A Company/Bn.

Gurner, Auguste - D Company/Rgt., Baltimore, 29. Died at the Natural Bridge, Mexico on 12/9/47.

Guy, James - F Company/Rgt., Baltimore, 18 (7/18/48).

Hackett, George W. - C Company/Rgt., Baltimore, 21 (4/30/48).

Hagedorn, Frederick - A Company/Rgt., Baltimore, 41. Died at the Natural Bridge, Mexico, regimental hospital on 10/6/47.

Haggerty, George W., Corporal - F Company/Rgt., Baltimore, 24 Discharged at Jalapa on 12/14/47.

Halderman, Jacob M., 2nd Sergeant - D Company/Rgt., Washington, 21 (2/29/48).

Hale, Caleb - A Company/Bn., Baltimore, 26 (5/30/47).

Ham, Anthony - G Company (Light Artillery)/Rgt., Baltimore, 25 (7/13/48).

Hamilton, John W. - F Company/Bn., Baltimore, 20 (5/30/46). Filed for pension from Maryland on 2/9/87, number S-2765.

Hands, Lafayette - F Company/Bn., Baltimore, 19 (5/30/46).

Hanison, Richard - B Company/Rgt., Washington, 19. Discharged by surgeon's certificate at Jalapa on 3/15/48.

Hanlon, Richard - F Company/Bn., Baltimore, 26 (5/30/46). Died and buried in Camargo, Mexico on 9/6/46. Printer, by trade and resident of Annapolis. (A-MS-1902) (B-10/16/46-1) (J-10/17/46-2)

Hanna, Lawrence - Recruit Company/Rgt., Baltimore, 39 (4/30/48).

Hanson, Washington C. - Recruit Company/Rgt., Baltimore. Wife, Elenora T., filed for pension from Maryland on 3/26/89, number W-7959.

Hardy, George - D Company/Rgt., Washington, 18 (2/29/48).

Harrighan, Thomas - Recruit Company/Rgt., Baltimore, 22. Discharged by surgeon's certificate from Fort McHenry on 3/18/48.

Harrington, Robert - B Company/Bn., Baltimore, 21 (5/30/46). Filed for pension from Maryland on 3/11/87, number S-2882. Soldier resided at 1211 Cross St., Baltimore in 1895. (L-9)

Harris, James - G Company (Light Artillery)/Rgt., Baltimore, 20 (7/13/48). Wife, Catherine, filed for pension from Maryland on 3/23/87, number W-868. Died prior to 1879. (L-9)

Harrison, John D. - F Company/Bn., Baltimore, 20 (5/30/46). Soldier filed for pension from Missouri on 5/5/87, number S-11675.

Harrison, William H. - H Company/Rgt., Washington, 31 (7/15/48). Wife, Mary Ann, filed for pension from Maryland on 3/7/87, number W-893. Also bounty land warrant, number 25,041-160-47.

Harrow, Columbus E. - B Company/Rgt., Washington. Wife, Isabella Celestia, filed for pension from the District of Columbia on 3/9/87, number W-891.

Hart, Albert - A Company/Bn., Baltimore, 41 (10/1/46). Discharged by surgeon's certificate due to severe wounds received at Monterey. Carried the colors at Monterey and as a result of his wounds, he had one arm amputated. (A-311)

MARYLAND AND D.C. VOLUNTEERS IN THE MEXICAN WAR

Hart, George - B Company/Rgt., Baltimore, 36 (8/17/48).

Harwood, Alexander H., 4th Sergeant - D Company/Rgt., Baltimore, 21. Died at Jalapa in quarters on 2/20/48.

Haslet, James - F Company/Bn., Baltimore, 18 (5/30/46).

Haslett, Robert E., 2nd Lieutenant - F Company/Bn., Baltimore, 22 (5/30/46).

Hassell, William F. - G Company (Light Artillery)/Rgt.

Hasselman, Taleman - C Company/Rgt., Baltimore, 26 (4/30/48).

Hatch, Julius - H Company/Rgt., Washington, 42 (7/15/48).

Hatch, William S. - E Company/Bn., Baltimore, 20 (12/31/46).

Haugh, Benjamin B. - G Company (Light Artillery)/Rgt., Baltimore, 24 (7/13/48).

Haupp, Casper - E Company/Rgt., Baltimore, 19 (7/18/48).

Hawkins, Barney - E Company/Bn., Baltimore. Discharged by surgeon's certificate on (8/31/46) at Camargo. (K-69)

Hax, Henry - E Company/Rgt., Baltimore, 19 (7/18/48).

Hax, Peter - E Company/Rgt., Baltimore, 19 (7/18/48).

Haxton, Columbus E. - B Company/Rgt., Washington, 23 (8/17/48).

Healey, George - E Company/Bn., Baltimore.

Hearst, Leonard C. - B Company/Bn., Baltimore.

Heckrotte, Henry W. - F Company/Bn., Baltimore, 20 (5/30/46). Died prior to 1879. (L-9)

Heft, Henry - E Company/Bn., Baltimore, 31 (12/31/46)

Heidelbach, Charles - E Company/Bn., Baltimore, 35 (12/31/46).

Hemming, Jacob - B Company/Bn., Baltimore. Slightly wounded at the Battle of Monterey on 9/21/46. (D-243)

Hemmrick, Jacob C., 2nd Lieutenant - C Company/Bn., Washington, Also served as a sergeant in H Company of the Regiment. Discharged by surgeon's certificate in Jalapa on 3/11/48.

Henderson, Armistead - E Company/Bn., Baltimore.

Henrie, Dan Drake, Captain - D Company/Rgt., Washington, 29 (2/29/48).

COMPENDIUM OF VOLUNTEERS

Henry, James - E Company/Bn., Baltimore, 33. Deserted near Castaneda on 12/15/46. Slightly wounded at the Battle of Monterey on 9/21/46. (D-243).

Henry, John D. - F Company/Bn., Baltimore, 22 (5/30/46). Wife, Emily C. Forest, filed for pension from Maryland on 10/19/89, number W-8446.

Henry, Richard P., 2nd Lieutenant - D Company/Rgt., Washington, 25 (2/29/48).

Henxler, Vincent - E Company/Bn., Baltimore, 23 (12/31/46).

Herman, Michael - F Company/Bn., Baltimore.

Herring, George A., Sergeant - F Company/Bn., Baltimore, 25 (5/30/46). Killed at the Battle of Monterey, 9/21/46. (A-MS-1902)

Hewitt, Albert - Regiment, Baltimore. Alias Ashel Hewitt. Filed for pension from Maryland on 3/25/91, number S-23420.

Heyer, Frederick - E Company/Rgt., Baltimore, 19. Discharged by surgeon's certificate at Vera Cruz on 1/9/48.

Heyn, Henry - C Company/Bn., Washington, 22 (2/28/47). Soldier filed for pension from Virginia on 3/9/87, number S-3058. Wife, Catherine, filed for pension from Maryland, number W-16857.

Hickman, William, Sergeant - E Company/Bn., Baltimore, 27 (12/31/46). Father was Colonel Nathaniel Hickman. (K-212)

Hilbert, Henry - G Company (Light Artillery)/Rgt., Baltimore, 19. Deserted from Fort McHenry on 9/6/47.

Hill, Charles - E Company/Bn., Baltimore. Soldier resided at 1809 E. Lombard St., Baltimore in 1893. (L-9)

Hill, George - C Company/Bn., Washington, 21 (2/28/47).

Hilleary, John W. - A Company/Rgt., Washington, 21 (7/24/48). Soldier filed for pension from Virginia on 3/21/87, number S-8556. Wife, Mary, filed for pension from the District of Columbia on 12/30/98, number W-14863.

Hiltz, John C. - A Company/Bn., Baltimore, 23 (5/30/47). Filed for pension from Maryland on 2/9/87, number S-3104. Soldier resided at 58 Cider Alley, Baltimore in 1887. (L-9)

Hindmans, William - C Company/Bn., Washington, 41 (2/28/47).

Hinds, Holiman H. - Recruit Company/Rgt., Baltimore, 18. Discharged by civil authority on 3/21/48.

Hisskins, John H. - E Company/Bn., Baltimore, 21 (12/31/46).

Hiver, John - C Company/Bn., Washington, 20 (2/28/47).

Hobbs, Beau H. - E Company/Rgt., Baltimore, 22. Discharged by surgeon's certificate at Vera Cruz on 12/14/47.

Hoff, Henry - B Company/Rgt., Baltimore, 23. Died at Jalapa in 1848.

Hoffman, John H. - E Company/Rgt., Baltimore. Discharged by surgeon's certificate in Jalapa on 3/14/48. Soldier filed for pension from Maryland on 3/22/87, number S-8576. Wife, Anna M., filed for pension from Maryland on 2/15/1907, number W-18619.

Hogan, William, 4th Corporal - F Company/Rgt., Baltimore, 20 (7/18/48).

Holen, Daniel H. - B Company/Rgt., Baltimore, 30 (8/17/48).

Holt, John William - E Company/Rgt., Baltimore, 27 (7/18/48). Wife, Julia, filed for pension from Maryland on 7/9/88, number W-6821.

Honiser, Alfred - B Company/Bn., Baltimore, 21 (5/30/46).

Hooper, John, 1st Lieutenant - C Company/Rgt., Baltimore.

Hooper, John - A Company/Bn., Baltimore, Transferred 6/1/46 as 2nd Master Sergeant in the Battalion Staff.

Hope, Thomas - F Company/Bn., Baltimore, 18 (5/30/46).

Hopkins, Dennis - G Company (Light Artillery)/Rgt., Baltimore, 32 (7/13/48).

Hopkins, J.T. - G Company (Light Artillery)/Rgt., Baltimore, 24 (7/13/48).

Hopper, Washington, 1st Lieutenant - E Company/Rgt., Baltimore, 25 (7/18/48).

Horan, Timothy - B Company/Bn., Baltimore, 30 (5/30/46).

Horn, John - E Company/Rgt., Baltimore, 42 Sick in hospital in Vera Cruz, died on 11/27/47 in hospital in New Orleans.

Horseler, Samuel C., Sergeant - B Company/Bn., Baltimore, 22 (5/30/46)

Houssanstopp, John - C Company/Bn., Washington, 30 (2/28/47).

Howard, Charles B. - A Company/Bn., Baltimore, 24 (5/30/47).

Howard, Clement W. - D Company/Bn., Washington. Filed for pension from Texas on 4/4/87, number S-8623. Died on 9/2/1914.

Howe, A.L. - Recruit Company/Rgt., Baltimore, 36 (4/30/48).

Howe, Edward - A Company/Rgt., Baltimore, 20 (7/24/48).

Howison, Alfred - B Company. Filed for pension from the District of Columbia on 5/17/88, number W-19406.

Hubner, Frederick - C Company/Rgt., Baltimore, 38 (4/30/48).

Hughes, Anthony - G Company (Light Artillery)/Rgt., Baltimore, 21 (7/13/48). Discharged by civil process.

Hughes, George W., Commanding Officer, Colonel. Wife, Ann Sarah, filed for pension from the District of Columbia on 4/21/87, number W-2940. Graduate of the Military Academy at West Point. He resigned from the army in 1851 and was elected to the U.S. Congress from Maryland. Following Congress, he returned to his estate on the West River and remained there until his death in 1871. (K-482)

Hughes, James - A Company/Bn., Baltimore, 19 (9/46). Discharged by surgeon's certificate.

Hughes, Joseph C. - D Company/Rgt., Baltimore, 39 (6/24/47).

Hughes, Thomas W. - H Company/Rgt., Baltimore. Discharged by surgeon's certificate at Jalapa on 2/48.

Hugo, George T. - E Company/Bn., Baltimore, 20 (12/31/46).

Hunold, George - B Company/Bn., Baltimore, 25 (5/30/46). Wife, Matilda, filed for pension from Pennsylvania on 3/23/95, number W-12643.

Hunter, Adam M. - F Company/Rgt., Baltimore, 21 (7/18/48). Soldier filed for pension, number S-18371. Wife, Jane, filed for pension from Maryland on 5/21/97, number W-13940.

Hunter, R. - G Company (Light Artillery)/Rgt., Baltimore, 19 (7/13/48).

Hunter, William S. - A Company/Bn., Baltimore, 23 (5/30/47).

Hurdle, Andrew Jackson - C Company/Bn., Washington, 19 (2/28/47). Filed for pension from the District of Columbia on 3/15/89, number S-21365.

Hurley, George W. - F Company/Rgt., Baltimore, 22. Discharged at Vera Cruz on 12/1/47. Filed for pension from Arkansas on 7/14/87, number S-15116.

Hurst, Leonard C. - B Company/Bn., Baltimore, 38 (5/30/46). Wife, Margaret, filed for pension from Maryland on 3/19/87, number W-1040.

Hurt, Barney - C Company/Bn., Washington, 26 (2/28/47).

Hutchings, William - E Company/Rgt., Baltimore. Deserted from Fort McHenry in the summer of 1847.

Hutchinson, William, Corporal - B Company/Rgt., Washington, 38 (8/17/48).

Huxford, Thomas J. - G Company (Light Artillery)/Rgt., Baltimore, 23. Deserted from Fort McHenry on 8/25/47.

Hyde, William S., Sergeant - A Company/Bn., Baltimore, Transferred to Battalion Staff as master sergeant on 12/7/46.

Hye, Ezekiell - A Company/Bn., Baltimore, 22 (5/30/47).

Ingle, Henry, 1st Sergeant - D Company/Bn., Washington, 30 (2/28/47). Also served in H Company of the Regiment. Wife, Elizabeth C., filed for pension from the District of Columbia on 2/11/89, number W-1054.

Irvin, James H. - F Company/Rgt., Baltimore, 20 (7/18/48). Wife, Kate, filed for pension from Maryland on 12/7/87, number W-5498. Soldier resided at 707 N. Calvert St., Baltimore until his death on 8/27/87. (L-10)

Irvin, Washington H. - D Company. Alias Wesley Hauptman. Filed for pension from Minnesota on 8/22/87, number S-16065.

Israel, James D. - G Company/Rgt. Wife, Emma, filed for pension from Louisiana on 12/29/87, number W-5627.

Jackson, Clarence - F Company/Bn., Baltimore, 26 (5/30/46). Soldier filed for pension from Louisiana on 2/4/88, number S-18413. Wife, Jane McC., filed for pension from Louisiana on 5/16/1901, number W-16204.

Jackson, John W., 2nd Corporal - A Company/Rgt., Washington, 31 (7/24/48).

Jackson, Samuel A. - D Company/Bn., Washington, 21 (2/28/47).

Jacobs, John - E Company/Rgt., Baltimore, 27 (7/18/48).

Jacobs, William

James, George - C Company/Rgt., Baltimore, 38 (4/30/48).

Jarrette, N. J. - E Company/Rgt., Baltimore.

Jarvis, Robert B., 1st Corporal - E Company/Rgt., Baltimore, 25 (7/18/48). Wife, Sarah E., filed for pension from Maryland on 2/15/87, number W-1076.

Jenkins, John J. - H Company/Rgt., Washington, 20 (7/15/48).

Jennings, Richard D. - Recruit Company/Rgt., Baltimore, 44 (2/29/48).

Jennings, Michael P. - Recruit Company/Rgt., Baltimore, 38 (2/29/48).

Jerrard, Owen - G Company (Light Artillery)/Rgt., Baltimore, 21 (7/13/48). Discharged by civil process.

Jervin, Washington H. - H Company/Rgt., Washington, 28 (7/15/48).

Johns, Walter R. - D Company/Bn., Washington, 18 (2/28/47). Soldier filed for pension from Pennsylvania on 1/18/92, number S-23792.

Johnson, Charles - E Company/Bn., Baltimore, 22 (12/31/46). Discharged by surgeon's certificate on (8/31/46) at Camargo. (K-69)

Johnson, David - E Company/Bn., Baltimore. Discharged by surgeon's certificate on (8/31/46) at Camargo. (K-69)

Johnson, Francis - A Company/Rgt., Washington, 22. Deserted from Fort McHenry on 7/10/47.

Johnson, James W. - B Company/Bn., Baltimore, 21 (5/30/46).

Johnson, John S. - E Company/Bn., Baltimore.

Johnson, John B., Musician - B Company/Bn., Baltimore, 32 (5/30/46).

Johnson, Matthew - F Company/Rgt., Baltimore, 19 (7/18/48). Soldier filed for pension from Virginia on 6/29/88, number S-19778. Wife, Betty S., filed for pension from Virginia on 4/5/1905, number W-18004.

Johnson, William - D Company/Rgt., Washington, 22 (2/29/48).

Johnson, William - F Company/Rgt., Baltimore, 28. Died at Vera Cruz in 11/47.

Jones, Alfred, Musician - D Company/Rgt., Washington, 21 (2/29/48).

Jones, G.R. - G Company (Light Artillery)/Rgt., Baltimore. Deserted.

Jones, Jacob - C Company/Bn., Washington, 24 (2/28/47).

Jones, John - E Company/Rgt., Baltimore.

Jones, Walter - A Company/Bn., Baltimore, 20 (5/30/47). Filed for pension from Maryland on 3/18/87, number S-8894.

Jones, William H. - A Company/Bn., Baltimore, 22 (5/30/47).

Jones, William T. - G Company (Light Artillery)/Rgt., Baltimore, 23 (7/13/48). Soldier filed for pension from Maryland on 2/7/87, number S-3551. Wife, Elizabeth R., filed for pension from Maryland on 6/4/1903, number W-17147.

Jordan, John - H Company/Rgt., Washington, 18 (7/15/48).

Jordan, John - A Company/Rgt., Washington, 42 (7/24/48).

Josephs, Abram - F Company/Rgt., Baltimore, 19 (7/18/48). Soldier filed for pension from Tennessee on 12/7/91, number S-23742.

Joyce, John T. - D Company/Bn., Washington, 22 (2/28/47).

Judy, George H., 4th Sergeant - D Company/Bn., Washington, 23 (2/28/47). Wife, Lizzie A., filed for pension from Maryland on 6/9/88, number W-6656.

Kaihart, Joseph - B Company/Bn., Baltimore, 25 (5/30/46).

Kammera, Henry - A Company/Rgt., Baltimore, 34 (7/24/48).

Kane, Robert - F Company/Bn., Baltimore, 18 (5/30/46). Soldier died prior to 1879. (L-11)

Kantner, John J., 2nd Sergeant - D Company/Bn., Washington, 24 (2/28/47). Soldier filed for pension from Maryland on 3/12/87, number S-3582. Wife, Susan E., filed for pension from Maryland on 12/20/90, number W-9529.

Kastine, Harman - C Company/Rgt., Baltimore, 26 (4/30/48).

Kasting, Augustus - C Company/Rgt., Baltimore, 33 (4/30/48).

Katzenberger, John - A Company/Rgt., Washington, 30 (7/24/48).

Kauffman, John Nicholas - E Company/Rgt., Baltimore. Soldier filed for pension from Maryland on 2/5/87, number S-3588.

Keenan, John F. - D Company/Rgt., Washington, 35 (2/29/48). Wife, Martha V., filed for pension from Delaware on 2/10/87, number W-1132.

Keenan, Thomas - D Company/Rgt., Philadelphia, 19 (2/29/48).

Keife, James - H Company/Rgt., Washington, 28 (7/15/48).

Keirle, Robert W. - B Company/Bn., Baltimore, 21 (5/30/46).

Keller, Charles - G Company (Light Artillery)/Rgt., Baltimore. Discharged by civil process.

Keller, Jesse, Corporal - A Company/Bn., Baltimore, 29 (5/30/47).

Kelly, Jackson - H Company/Rgt., Baltimore, 21 (7/15/48).

Kelly, James, Corporal - A Company/Rgt., Washington, 21 Accidentally drowned near Louisville, Kentucky on 7/13/48.

Kelly, James - G Company (Light Artillery)/Rgt., Baltimore, 21. Deserted from Fort McHenry on 9/2/47.

Kelly, John - A Company/Rgt., Washington, 45 (7/24/48).

Kelly, John W. - G Company (Light Artillery)/Rgt., Baltimore, 19. Deserted from Fort McHenry on 9/9/47, apprehended 3/20/48. Deserted again on 3/21/48, apprehended on 4/26/48.

Kelly, Thaddeus - D Company/Bn., Washington, 22 (2/28/47). Soldier filed for pension from Maryland on 6/7/88, number S-18107.

Kelly, Thomas - F Company/Rgt., Baltimore, 20 (7/18/48).

Kelly, William - F Company/Bn., Baltimore, 24 (5/30/46). Severely wounded at the Battle of Monterey on 9/21/46. (D-243)

Kemp, Andrew, Corporal - C Company/Bn., Washington, Elected 1st Corporal in Washington City. (N-5/20/46-1)

Kendall, Charles - E Company/Rgt., Baltimore, 23. Died in Jalapa on April 8, 1848.

Kendig, Benjamin F. - Recruit Company/Rgt., Baltimore, 18. (4/30/48).

Kenly, John Reese, Commanding Officer, Captain - E Company/Bn., Baltimore. Born in 1822. Later served as Major and executive officer on the Regimental Staff. His parents were Edward Kenly, whose family originally settled in Harford County, and a Miss Reese (originally spelled Rhys in Wales), whose family were members of the Society of Friends, from Baltimore. John Kenly was educated in private schools in the City and after studying law under the McCulloh and Buchanan's practice, joined the Bar in 1845. Following the Mexican War, he was defeated in his attempt to become U.S. Congressman from the Fourth District, Maryland. He resumed his law practice in Baltimore residing at 56 Fayette Street until the beginning of the Civil War. During the Civil War, Kenly served with distinction attaining the rank of Brevet Major-General while commanding the Maryland Brigade and the 1st Maryland Regiment. Before his death, he resided at 617 West Baltimore Street.

Died on 12/20/91, unmarried. Buried at Greenmount Cemetery in Baltimore. (C-1845) (F-219) (O-588)

Kennedy, George W. - F Company/Rgt., Baltimore, 20 (7/18/48).

Kennedy, William B., 3rd Corporal - G Company (Light Artillery)/Rgt., Baltimore, 19 (7/13/48).

Kenny, John - E Company/Rgt., Baltimore, 22. Deserted from Fort McHenry in the summer of 1847.

Kenny, Mathew - E Company/Rgt., Baltimore, 23 (7/18/48).

Kernin, Joseph - G Company (Light Artillery)/Rgt.

Kidd, William (P. or J. or G.) - F Company/Rgt., Baltimore, 18 (7/18/48). Wife, Mary E., filed for pension from Indiana on 3/11/99, number W-14986.

Kierle, Robert W., Corporal - B Company/Bn. Filed for pension from Virginia on 2/10/87, number S-3676.

Kimp, Andrew - C Company/Bn., Washington, 21 (2/28/47).

King, Thomas - D Company/Bn., Washington, 20 (2/28/47). Served as 1st Corporal in H Company of the Regiment.

Klassen, Jacob S. - F Company/Bn., Baltimore, 19 (5/30/46). Later served as 1st Lieutenant in the F Company of the Regiment.

Kline, Godfrey - F Company/Bn., Baltimore, 21 (5/30/46).

Klockgether, William - A Company/Bn., Baltimore, 22 (5/30/47).

Kloman, Charles - C Company/Rgt., Baltimore, 26 (4/30/48). Wife, Louisia, filed for pension from the District of Columbia on 5/16/88, number W-6511.

Klopfer, Frederick A., 1st Lieutenant - D Company/Rgt., Washington, 33 (2/29/48). Soldier filed for pension from the District of Columbia on 5/9/87, number S-12506.

Knight, Henry - D Company/Bn., Washington.

Knight, James - E Company/Rgt., Baltimore. Died at Vera Cruz on October 6, 1847.

Knight, Leroy - E Company/Bn., Baltimore.

Kniminick, John - E Company/Rgt., Baltimore, 42 (7/18/48). Died at the Natural Bridge in Mexico.

Knott, Joseph - C Company/Bn., Washington, 35 (2/28/47).

Knott, Walter D. - G Company (Light Artillery)/Rgt., Baltimore, 29 (7/13/48).

Koch, Martin - E Company/Rgt., Baltimore. Alias Martin Kaufman. Filed for pension from the District of Columbia on 4/1/87, number S-8992.

Kounselman, Frederick - C Company/Rgt., Baltimore, 32 (4/30/48)

Kraft, Edward B., 4th Sergeant - C Company/Rgt., Baltimore, 32 (4/30/48). Soldier filed for pension from Virginia in 1887, number S-3763.

Kraft, Michael - B Company/Bn., Baltimore, 22 (5/30/46).

Kraft, William - E Company/Rgt., Baltimore, 31. Deserted from Fort McHenry on 6/30/47.

Kreamer, George - G Company (Light Artillery)/Rgt.

Krebs, James - H Company/Rgt., Baltimore, 19 (7/15/48).

Krusp, Thomas - G Company (Light Artillery)/Rgt., Baltimore, 33 (7/13/48).

Kuhnes, Joseph - A Company/Bn., Baltimore, 19 (5/30/47).

Kump, Joseph - H Company/Rgt., Washington. Died at the regimental hospital in 1848.

Kurtz, Thomas, Corporal - H Company/Rgt., Washington, 23 (7/15/48). Soldier filed for pension from the District of Columbia on 5/16/87, number S-12542. Wife, Martha, filed for pension from Indiana on 9/29/98, number W-14753.

Labedie, Francis A. - E Company/Bn., Baltimore.

Lancaster, George W. - H Company/Rgt., Baltimore, 18 (7/15/48).

Lane, Charles - G Company (Light Artillery)/Rgt., Baltimore, 19 (7/13/48).

Lane, Michael - F Company/Bn., Baltimore, 23 (5/30/46).

Langdon, Charles W. - D Company/Bn., Washington. Wife, Clara filed for pension from New York on 10/26/97, W-14221.

Lanham, Jonathan - A Company/Rgt., Washington, 24 (7/24/48).

Lank, Nicholas B., 4th Sergeant - E Company/Rgt., Baltimore, 28 (7/18/48).

Lanman, Josias - E Company/Rgt., Baltimore.

Lansdale, George Oliver, Sergeant - E Company/Bn., Baltimore, 27 (12/31/46)

Laughlin, Samuel H. - A Company/Rgt., Baltimore, 21 Dishonorably discharged on 2/3/48.

Laugton, Samuel W., 3rd Sergeant - A Company/Rgt., Washington, 18 (7/24/48).

Lawn, John - F Company/Bn., Baltimore, 32 (5/30/46).

Lawrence, George - C Company/Bn., Washington, 36 (2/28/47).

Ledoger, John B. - E Company/Rgt., Baltimore, 29. Deserted from Fort McHenry in the summer of 1847.

Lee, Edward F. - G Company (Light Artillery)/Rgt., Baltimore, 26 (7/13/48). Died prior to 1879. (L-12)

Lee, William - A Company/Bn., Baltimore, 22 (5/30/47). Very severely wounded at the Battle of Monterey on 9/21/46. Soldier filed for pension from Maryland on 6/7/87, S-13885. Wife, Josephine V., filed from Maryland on 8/13/1900, W-15747. Resided in Bel Air, Maryland in 1891. (D-243) (L-12)

Leeson, Maurice C. - G Company/Rgt., Baltimore. Soldier filed for pension from Maryland on 3/23/87, S-9061. Wife, Rachel S., filed for pension from Maryland on 2/26/92, W-10435. Resided at 819 W. Lexington St., Baltimore until his death on 12/18/91. (L-12).

Leitch, Andrew J. - H Company/Rgt., Washington, 18 (7/15/48).

Lennox, William, Musician - H Company/Rgt., Baltimore. Discharged by surgeon's certificate at Jalapa on 3/14/48.

Lennox, William T., Sgt. Major - A Company/Bn., Baltimore, Appointed sergeant major of the Battalion on 2/16/47. He also served at standard bearer for the Battalion.

Leventon, Thomas - E Company/Bn., Baltimore, 26 (12/31/46).

Lewis, Edward - B Company/Rgt., Washington, 36 (8/17/48).

Lewis, William - see Dulaney, William S.

Lewscomb, Jacob - E Company/Rgt., Baltimore.

Leyburn, Thomas - E Company/Bn., Baltimore, 18 (12/31/46).

Lickey, James - G Company (Light Artillery)/Rgt., Baltimore, 25 (7/13/48).

COMPENDIUM OF VOLUNTEERS   47

Lightner, William - A Company/Bn., Baltimore, 21 (11/22/46). Discharged by surgeon's certificate due to disability at Monterey.

Liles, William - C Company/Bn., Washington, 31 (2/28/47).

Link, William B. - E Company/Rgt., Baltimore, 21. Deserted from Fort McHenry in the summer of 1847.

Little, John - H Company/Rgt., Baltimore. Soldier filed for pension from Indiana on 2/4/84, S-4114. Wife, Malinda J., filed for pension from Indiana on 6/28/1917, W-20482. Bounty Land Warrant #16510-160-47.

Lloyd, John T. - F Company/Rgt., Baltimore, 26 (7/18/48).

Lloyd, Joshua - H Company/Rgt., Baltimore. Discharged at Fort McHenry on 10/14/47.

Locke, John H., Corporal - D Company/Rgt., Washington, 26 (2/29/48). Soldier filed for pension from the District of Columbia on 2/4/87, S-4131.

Lockhart, Samuel - E Company/Bn., Baltimore. Discharged by surgeon's certificate on (8/31/46) at Camargo. (K-69)

Lockhears, Josiah - D Company/Rgt., Philadelphia, 20. Discharged by surgeon's certificate at Vera Cruz general hospital on 1/10/48.

Logan, Alexander - B Company/Bn., Baltimore, 32 (5/30/46).

Longerback, Frederick - C Company/Bn., Washington, 24 (2/28/47).

Losekamp, Jacob - E Company/Bn., Baltimore. Soldier filed for pension from Montana Territory on 3/1/87, S-11166.

Loughry, John - E Company/Bn., Baltimore.

Lount, Winslow - B Company/Rgt., Washington, 28 (8/17/48).

Love, John A. - G Company (Light Artillery)/Rgt., Baltimore, 20 (4/30/48). Discharged by civil process. Soldier filed for pension from Maryland on 3/9/88, S-18740. Wife, Amy E., filed for pension from Maryland on 2/15/1911, W-19721. Resided at 317 N. Carey St., Baltimore in 1896. (L-12).

Love, Samuel C. - A Company/Bn., Baltimore, 21 (5/30/47). Soldier filed for pension from Virginia on 2/18/87, S-4174. Resided at 1134 N. Woodyear St., Baltimore in 1895. (L-12)

Lovell, George - G Company (Light Artillery)/Rgt., Baltimore, 25 (7/13/48). Soldier filed for pension from Maryland on 4/14/87, S-11032.

Lovell, William - F Company/Bn., Baltimore, 32 (5/30/46).

Lucas, Thomas - Recruit Company/Rgt., Baltimore, 22 (2/29/48).

Ludwig, Francis - E Company/Rgt., Baltimore, 34 (7/18/48).

Luidie, Henry B. - A Company/Rgt., Baltimore, 25 (7/24/48).

Luson, Morrison - G Company (Light Artillery)/Rgt., Baltimore, 24 (7/13/48).

Luxson, Joseph - C Company/Bn., Washington, 23 (2/28/47).

Mabbett, Ira, 2nd Lieutenant - C Company/Rgt., Baltimore, During April, 1848, on sick furlough. Also served as commander of the recruiting party at Fort McHenry. Soldier filed for pension from Arizona Territory on 6/25/88, S-19749.

Macbeth, John - A Company/Rgt., Baltimore, 27 (7/24/48).

Mackey, James C. - H Company/Rgt., Baltimore. Soldier filed for pension, S-9176. Wife, Sidney J., filed for pension from Pennsylvania on 11/19/1901, W-16430.

Macnelly, George - E Company/Bn., Baltimore, 30 (12/31/46)

Macready, William - E Company/Bn., Baltimore. Discharged by surgeon's certificate on (8/31/46) at Camargo. (K-69)

Magee, William - D Company/Rgt., Philadelphia, 27 (2/29/48).

Magness, John - E Company/Bn., Baltimore, 19 (12/31/46).

Magruder, Gabriel - A Company/Rgt., Washington, 20 (7/24/48).

Mahone, Roger J. - F Company/Bn., Baltimore, 20 (5/30/46). Died prior to 1879. (L-13)

Major, James C. - A Company/Bn., Baltimore, 37 (5/30/47).

Mallory, Wallace F. - F Company/Bn., Baltimore, 20 (5/30/46).

Manning, Martin - G Company (Light Artillery)/Rgt., Baltimore. Discharged by civil process.

Manning, Thomas, 3rd Corporal - H Company/Rgt., Baltimore, 23 (7/15/48).

Mannion, Joseph - F Company/Rgt., Baltimore, 26 (7/18/48).

Mansfield, James H., Corporal - E Company/Bn., Baltimore, 25 (12/31/46). Served as a 2nd Sergeant in H Company of the Regiment.

Markam, Francis - A Company/Rgt., Washington, 35 (7/24/48).

Marrow, Isaac H., 1st Lieutenant - G Company (Light Artillery)/Rgt., Baltimore, 22 (7/13/48). Soldier filed for pension from the District of Columbia on 5/14/87, S-10069. Wife, Elizabeth E., filed for pension from Illinois on 6/7/1912, W-19968. Also served as an officer in the 3rd Ohio Volunteer Regiment during the Civil War. (G)

Martin, James - D Company/Bn., Washington, 19 (2/28/47). Soldier filed for pension from Louisiana on 3/16/87, S-9208.

Martin, John - E Company/Rgt., Baltimore, 38 (7/18/48).

Martin, Joseph - A Company/Bn., Baltimore, 26 8/46. Discharged by surgeon's certificate at Camp Belknap.

Martine, George - G Company (Light Artillery)/Rgt., Baltimore, 20 (7/13/48). Discharged by civil process.

Mason, Edward W. - F Company/Rgt., Baltimore, 21. Discharged at New Orleans.

Matchett, Charles W. - E Company/Bn., Baltimore, 20 (12/31/46).

Matthews, John H., 2nd Corporal - G Company (Light Artillery)/Rgt., Baltimore, 23 (7/13/48).

McBrafly, John - D Company/Rgt., Baltimore, 20 (2/29/48).

McCain, James - F Company/Rgt., Baltimore, 18. Discharged at Jalapa on 12/1/47.

McCeney, Zacharia - G Company (Light Artillery)/Rgt., Baltimore, 34 (7/13/48). Soldier filed for pension from Maryland on 3/29/87, S-9283.

McClane, George W., 2nd Corporal - F Company/Rgt., Baltimore, 22 (7/18/48).

McConnell, John - D Company/Rgt., Baltimore, 21 (2/29/48). Soldier filed for pension from Pennsylvania on 3/18/87, S-9286.

McCormick, John - E Company/Rgt., Baltimore, 26. Deserted from Fort McHenry in the summer of 1847.

McCormick, William - B Company/Bn., Baltimore, 28 (5/30/46).

McCormick, William - G Company (Light Artillery)/Rgt., Baltimore, 26 (7/13/48).

McCourt, John - B Company/Bn., Baltimore, 24 (5/30/46).

McCoy, William - B Company/Rgt., Washington, 25. Discharged by surgeon's certificate at Jalapa on 3/15/48.

McDonald, James A. - B Company/Rgt., Washington. Died at the Natural Bridge, Mexico in 1847.

McElwee, William, Artificer - G Company (Light Artillery)/Rgt., Baltimore, 20 (7/13/48). Soldier filed for pension from Maryland on 2/10/87, S-9311.

McEnroe, James - G Company (Light Artillery)/Rgt.

McGee, Daniel K. - G Company (Light Artillery)/Rgt., Baltimore, 23 (7/13/48). Wife, Mary M., filed for pension from Iowa on 11/8/87, W-5271.

McGinley, John - D Company/Rgt., Philadelphia, 20 (2/29/48). Soldier filed for pension from Pennsylvania on 4/6/88, S-19006.

McGreggor, John J. - A Company/Rgt., Baltimore, 36 (7/24/48).

McGunnell, John - E Company/Bn., Baltimore. Missing during march to Matamoras. (K-38)

McIntire, James H., 3rd Corporal - F Company/Bn., Baltimore, 22 (5/30/46).

McKeldin, David W. - F Company/Bn., Baltimore, 19 (5/30/46).

McKenzie, William - G Company (Light Artillery)/Rgt., Baltimore, 24 (7/13/48).

McLaughlin, James - F Company/Rgt., Baltimore, 20 (7/18/48). Soldier filed for pension from Virginia on 1/16/89, S-21050. Wife, Ann M., filed for pension from Maryland on 2/1/95, W-12540. Resided at the Hygeria Hotel, Norfolk, Virginia until his death in 1894. (L-13)

McLaughlin, John - C Company/Bn., Washington, 33 (2/28/47).

McLaughlin, Thomas - B Company/Rgt., Washington, 22 (8/17/48).

McLean, James Jr., 1st Lieutenant - H Company/Rgt., Baltimore. Wife, Mary E., filed for pension from California on 2/11/87, W-1521.

McMackin, Robert - F Company/Bn., Baltimore, 20 (5/30/46). Deserted.

McMarr, John - G Company (Light Artillery)/Rgt., Baltimore, 26 (7/13/48).

McNaughton, Lawrence - B Company/Rgt., Washington, 31 (8/17/48). Wife, Mary B., filed for pension from the District of Columbia on 1/14/89, W-5729.

COMPENDIUM OF VOLUNTEERS   51

McNeal, William - F Company/Bn., Baltimore, 21 (5/30/46).

McNeil, John W. - A Company/Bn., Baltimore, 29 (8/28/46).
  Discharged by surgeon's certificate at Camp Belknap.

McNeir, Joseph R. - B Company/Bn., Baltimore, 21 (5/30/46).

McPherson, William - C Company/Bn., Washington, 28 (2/28/47).

McPolan, Thomas - C Company/Rgt., Baltimore, 19 (4/30/48).

Mead, Patrick - E Company/Rgt., Baltimore.

Mearis, Leonard - F Company/Bn., Baltimore, 19 (5/30/46).

Meeks, Allen - G Company (Light Artillery)/Rgt., Baltimore, 23 (7/13/48).

Merritt, William C. - A Company/Bn., Baltimore, 23 (9/46).
  Discharged by surgeon's certificate at Camargo.

Merton, James H. - E Company/Bn., Baltimore, 27 (12/31/46).

Messick, James, Corporal - A Company/Bn., Baltimore, 29 (5/30/47).

Meteer, Andrew - F Company/Bn., Baltimore, 20 (5/30/46).

Meyer, John - C Company/Rgt., Baltimore, 36 (4/30/48). Wife, Eliza A., filed for pension from Pennsylvania on 4/25/87, W-3013.

Meyers, George - E Company/Bn., Baltimore. Soldier filed for pension from Ohio on 5/23/87, S-13327.

Michael, George W. - Bn. Wife, Marian J., filed for pension from Ohio on 10/31/88, W-7326.

Miffitt, Joseph - H Company/Rgt., Jalapa, Mexico.

Milbourn, Timothy, Corporal - B Company/Rgt., Washington, 48 (8/17/48).

Miles, Smythe M., Surgeon of the Battalion. Native of Georgia, became surgeon on 8/8/46.

Millard, Joseph B. - E Company/Bn., Baltimore, 21 (12/31/46).

Miller, Edward - F Company/Rgt., Baltimore, 21 (7/18/48).

Miller, Henry - A Company/Rgt., Baltimore, 33 (7/24/48).

Miller, Jacob - Recruit Company/Rgt., Baltimore, 26 (2/29/48).

Miller, Jacob S. - D Company/Rgt., Philadelphia, 19 (2/29/48). Soldier filed for pension from Pennsylvania on 6/13/88, S-19654. Wife, Annie E., filed for pension from Pennsylvania on 10/15/94, W-12353.

Miller, John - C Company/Bn., Washington. Soldier filed for pension from Kentucky on 5/13/87, S-12604.

Mills, Thomas W. - G Company (Light Artillery)/Rgt., Baltimore, 20 (7/13/48). Soldier filed for pension from Maryland on 2/11/88, S-18472. Resided at 11 Barclay Street, Baltimore in 1889. (L-13)

Milnor, Henry M., 2nd Lieutenant - G Company (Light Artillery)/Rgt., Baltimore, 24 (7/13/48).

Milstead, William - C Company/Bn., Washington, 18 (2/28/47).

Misler, Josiah - D Company/Rgt., Washington, 19 (2/29/48).

Mitchell, Charles - B Company/Bn., Baltimore, 30 (5/30/46).

Mitchell, Francis J. - Recruit Company/Rgt., Baltimore, 22 (2/29/48).

Mitchell, George - G Company (Light Artillery)/Rgt., Baltimore, 33 (7/13/48).

Mitchell, Hooper - A Company/Bn.

Mitchell, John - B Company/Bn., Baltimore, 18 (5/30/46).

Moller, John H.F. - A Company/Rgt., Washington, 18 (7/24/48). Alias Nicholas J. Moller. Soldier filed for pension from Georgia on 3/1/87, S-4709. Wife, Anna M., filed for pension from Georgia on 12/19/1906, W-18569.

Monroe, John - C Company/Rgt., Baltimore, 22 (4/30/48).

Moore, J.M. - G Company (Light Artillery)/Rgt., Baltimore, 25 (7/13/48).

Moore, John - D Company/Rgt., Washington, 23 (2/29/48).

Moran, A.F. - G Company (Light Artillery)/Rgt., Baltimore, 32 (7/13/48).

Moran, James - D Company/Bn., Washington, 20 (2/28/47).

Moran, John - B Company/Rgt., Washington, 22 (8/17/48).

Moran, John - A Company/Bn., Baltimore, 30 (5/30/47). Also served in H Company of the Regiment. Soldier filed for pension from Maryland on 2/14/87, S-4791.

Moran, Owen - B Company/Bn., Baltimore, 30 (5/30/46).

Moran, Thomas - B Company/Rgt., Washington, 36 (8/17/48).

Morgan, John - A Company/Bn., Baltimore, 19 (5/30/47).

Morrell, Edward - F Company/Bn., Baltimore, 26 (5/30/46).

Morris, Jacob - E Company/Bn., Baltimore.

Morris, Thomas P. - B Company/Bn., Baltimore, 18 (5/30/46). Wife, Grace A., filed for pension from Maryland on 2/11/87, W-1421.

Morrow, Henry A. - C Company/Bn., Washington, 18 (2/28/47).

Morrow, Isaac H., 1st Lieutenant - B Company/Bn., Baltimore,

Morse, Augustus S. - F Company/Rgt., Baltimore, 22 (7/18/48). Alias Stephen A. Morse. Soldier filed for pension from Maryland on 2/24/87, S-9602. Wife, Sarah A., filed for pension from Maryland on 1/31/98, W-14381.

Morton, Charles D. - B Company/Bn., Baltimore, 18 (5/30/46).

Morton, William - B Company/Bn., Baltimore, 22 (5/30/46).

Moses, Elizur - A Company/Rgt. Soldier filed for pension from New York on 2/15/87, S-4800.

Mount, John W., 1st Sergeant - C Company/Bn., Washington, Elected 1st Sergeant in Washington City. (N-5/20/46-1).

Mount, Thomas - C Company/Bn., Washington, 18 (2/28/47).

Mullen, James, 1st Sergeant - B Company/Bn., Baltimore, 21 (5/30/46). Wife, Mary A., filed for pension from Maryland on 2/21/87, W-1446.

Mullen, James Jr. - B Company/Bn., Baltimore, 23 (5/30/46).

Mulloy, John J., 2nd Lieutenant - H Company/Rgt., Baltimore, Resigned on 2/6/48.

Murdoch, Gilbert, 3rd Corporal - F Company/Rgt., Baltimore, 22 (7/18/48). Wife, Eleanor J., filed for pension from Pennsylvania on 9/10/87, W-4796.

Murphy, Daniel - C Company/Rgt., Baltimore, 30 (4/30/48). Soldier filed for pension from Maryland on 2/26/87, S-4846. Wife, Martha, filed for pension from Maryland on 11/1/99, W-15357. Resided at 1329 N. Broadway, Baltimore in 1895. (L-13)

Murphy, Edward, 2nd Lieutenant - D Company/Bn., Washington. Soldier filed for pension from Missouri on 12/1/88, S-20798.

Wife, Mary, filed for pension from Illinois on 7/24/99, W-15204.

Murphy, Lambert T. - Recruit Company/Rgt., Baltimore, 28 (2/29/48). Deserted from Fort McHenry on 3/15/48, apprehended on 3/20/48.

Murray, David G., 2nd Sergeant - G Company (Light Artillery)/Rgt., Baltimore, 27 (7/13/48). Soldier filed for pension from Maryland on 2/13/87, S-4848. Resided at 623 Columbia Ave., Baltimore in 1895.

Murray, Frank J. - F Company/Rgt., Baltimore, 22. Died at Puente Nacional, Mexico on 10/12/47.

Murray, Rufus, Corporal - D Company/Rgt., Baltimore, 26. Died at Jalapa in the regimental hospital on 2/26/48.

Murtuck, William - H Company/Rgt., Baltimore. Discharged due to age (minor) on 10/15/47.

Myer, George W. - B Company/Rgt., Washington, 28 (8/17/48). Died prior to 1879. (L-13)

Myerhoffer, Peter, Sergeant - B Company/Rgt., Washington, 42. Died at the National Bridge, Mexico on 10/20/47.

Myers, Charles F. H. - B Company/Rgt., Washington. Died at Vera Cruz in 1847.

Myers, Edward - E Company/Bn., Baltimore, 34 (12/31/46). Wife, Mary E., filed for pension from Maryland on 3/17/87, W-1461.

Nack, William - F Company/Bn., Baltimore, 20 (5/30/46).

Nalley, William H., 2nd Sergeant - A Company/Rgt., Washington, 29 (7/24/48). Soldier filed for pension from the District of Columbia on 3/4/87, S-3795.

Neidhamer, John, 4th Corporal - C Company/Rgt., Baltimore, 39 (4/30/48).

Nettan, Francis Louis - E Company/Bn., Baltimore, 23 (12/31/46). Alias Louis Netter. Soldier filed for pension from Wisconsin on 2/26/87, S-3834. Wife, Ida, filed for pension from Wisconsin on 12/14/1903, W-17393.

Nibling, Henry - H Company/Rgt., Baltimore, 20 (7/15/48).

Nichols, Isaac, Corporal - B Company/Bn., Baltimore, 25 (5/30/46).

Nichols, William J. - F Company/Rgt., Baltimore, 22 (7/18/48). Wife, Sarah A, filed for pension from Maryland on 4/16/87, W-

2588. Resided at Waverly in Baltimore until his death on 8/5/86. (L-14)

Nicholson, E.J., Corporal - G Company (Light Artillery)/Rgt., Baltimore, 37 (7/13/48). Died.

Nimmocks, Leonard - B Company/Rgt., Washington, 34. Discharged by surgeon's certificate at Fort McHenry on 7/10/47.

Nimocks, Franklin B. - E Company/Bn., Baltimore, 22 (12/31/46). Later served as a 2nd Lieutenant in Company F/Bn. Wife, Mary E., filed for pension from Pennsylvania on 6/1/87, W-3515.

Norturman, Henry B. - C Company/Rgt., Baltimore, 23 (4/30/48).

Norris, Andrew J. - D Company/Bn., Washington, 47 (2/28/47). Slightly wounded at the Battle of Monterey on 9/21/46. (D-243)

Norris, Henry P. - E Company/Bn., Baltimore, 27 (12/31/46). Resident of Baltimore, killed a man in the quartermaster department on 5/30/47. He was found guilty and sentenced to prison. Pleas from Captain Kenly and the Battalion were sustained and Norris was eventually released. (K-273)

Northerman, Henry B. - B Company/Bn., Baltimore, 22 (5/30/46).

Norwood, John E. - G Company (Light Artillery)/Rgt., Baltimore, 18 (7/13/48). Soldier filed for pension from Maryland on 2/10/87, S-3896. Wife, Wilhelmine C., filed for pension from Maryland on 10/4/1912, W-20006.

O'Brien, James, 2nd Lieutenant - E Company/Rgt., Baltimore, 23 (7/18/48). Wife, Annie R., filed for pension from Maryland on 3/14/87, W-1587.

O'Brien, Patrick - B Company/Bn., Baltimore, 22 (5/30/46). Killed in action in the Battle of Monterey on 9/21/46. (D-241)

O'Brien, Thomas - Battalion. Wife, Mary, filed for pension from Maryland on 1/21/89, W-7607.

O'Brien, William, 2nd Lieutenant - C Company/Bn., Washington. In 1846, he resided at the corner of 13th and D Streets NW. (W-1846).

O'Keefe, Francis B. - D Company/Rgt., Philadelphia, 18 (2/29/48).

O'Leary, Cornelius - B Company/Bn., Baltimore, 45 (5/30/46).

O'Mealley, Thomas - G Company (Light Artillery)/Rgt., Baltimore, 25 (7/13/48).

Ogden, John H. - D Company/Bn., Washington, 23 (2/28/47). Wife, Isabella D., filed for pension from Maryland on 4/9/87, W-1594.

MARYLAND AND D.C. VOLUNTEERS IN THE MEXICAN WAR

Oneil, James - E Company/Rgt., Baltimore, 24 (7/18/48).

Osbourn, John - B Company/Rgt., Washington. Died at New Orleans on 12/27/47.

Othick, Henry - G Company (Light Artillery)/Rgt., Baltimore, 21. Deserted from Fort McHenry on 9/2/47.

Owen, Benjamin F., 1st Lieutenant - A Company/Bn., Baltimore, Resigned (2/27/47).

Owens, David - C Company/Rgt., Baltimore, 20 (4/30/48).

Pactoleto, Lorant - G Company (Light Artillery)/Rgt., Baltimore, 25 (7/13/48).

Page, William - H Company/Rgt., Baltimore, 26 (7/15/48). Wife, Catherine E., filed for pension from Maryland on 3/22/87, W-1651.

Palmer, William - B Company/Rgt., Washington, 42 (8/17/48). Wife, Ellen, filed for pension from the District of Columbia on 2/18/87, W-1626.

Parham, William J., 1st Lieutenant - D Company/Bn., Washington. Wife, Martha, filed for pension from the District of Columbia on 2/18/87, W-1643.

Parkhill, Hamilton - E Company/Rgt., Baltimore, 32 (7/18/48).

Parlette, William A. - A Company/Bn., Baltimore, 31 (9/46). Discharged by surgeon's certificate at Camargo.

Parras, Joseph - G Company (Light Artillery)/Rgt., Baltimore, 36 (7/13/48). Died.

Parsons, Joseph, Corporal - B Company/Rgt., Washington, 28. Died at Jalapa on 1/11/48.

Payne, Elisha R. - H Company/Rgt., Baltimore. Discharged by surgeon's certificate at Jalapa on 6/48.

Payne, John - D Company/Bn., Washington, 22 (2/28/47). Soldier filed for pension from Virginia on 2/5/87, S-5073.

Pearson, George W. - F Company/Bn., Baltimore, 29 (5/30/46). Died of disease at Monterey. Resident of Baltimore. (K-172)

Pease, William - G Company (Light Artillery)/Rgt., Baltimore, 20. Deserted from Fort McHenry on 9/3/47.

Pease, William H. - D Company/Rgt., Washington, 26 (2/29/48).

Peastner, William - C Company/Bn., Washington, 20 (2/28/47).

Peck, Charles - D Company/Bn., Washington, Slightly wounded at the Battle of Monterey on 9/21/46. (D-243)

Penn, Jacob W. - A Company/Rgt., Washington, 35 (7/24/48).

Penn, Thomas, 1st Corporal - A Company/Rgt., Washington, 26 (7/24/48).

Perdigue, Francis - B Company/Bn., Baltimore, 19 (5/30/46).

Perdue, John - F Company/Rgt., Baltimore, 18 (7/18/48).

Peregoy, James - E Company/Bn., Baltimore. Discharged by surgeon's certificate on (8/31/46) at Camargo. Soldier filed for pension from Maryland on 6/6/87, S-14284. (K-69)

Peterson, William - B Company/Bn., Baltimore,

Petherbridge, Edward R., 1st Sergeant - G Company (Light Artillery)/Rgt., Baltimore, 25 (7/13/48). Soldier filed for pension from Maryland on 4/14/87, S-11073. Wife, Sarah A., filed for pension from Maryland on 8/16/1904, W-17743. Soldier also served in the Purnell Legion, Maryland Volunteers, in the Civil War.

Phaef, John M. - B Company/Rgt., Baltimore, 35 (8/17/48).

Phelps, William C. - A Company/Bn., Baltimore, 21 (5/30/47). Soldier filed for pension from Delaware on 4/9/87, S-9818. Wife, Tamar J., filed for pension from Delaware on 3/7/1904, W-17509.

Pierce, John, Corporal - D Company/Bn., Washington, 24 (2/28/47).

Pierpoint, Amoss - E Company/Rgt., Baltimore, 32 (7/18/48).

Pierpoint, John - E Company/Rgt., Baltimore, 36 (7/18/48).

Piles, James - A Company/Bn., Baltimore, Very severely wounded at the Battle of Monterey on 9/21/46. (D-243)

Pim, John P. - F Company/Rgt., Baltimore, 21 (7/18/48).

Pindle, William T. - C Company/Rgt., Baltimore, 23 (4/30/48). Soldier filed for pension from Maryland on 2/26/87, S-5189.

Pingle, Henry - C Company/Bn., Washington, 19 (2/28/47).

Pioneer, William H., Musician - B Company/Bn., Baltimore, 23 (5/30/46)

Piper, James S., Commanding Officer, Captain - B Company/Bn., Baltimore. Soldier filed for pension from Arkansas on 2/4/87,

58   MARYLAND AND D.C. VOLUNTEERS IN THE MEXICAN WAR

S-5191. Wife, Mary Ann, filed for pension from Arkansas on 1/29/89, W-7640.

Plowman, Alfred J. - F Company/Bn., Baltimore, 22 (5/30/46).

Plummer, James H. - F Company/Bn., Baltimore, 22 (5/30/46). Soldier filed for pension from Maryland on 1/7/88, S-18113.

Poinier, William H. - B Company/Bn., Baltimore. Soldier filed for pension from Colorado on 2/4/87, S-5216.

Polly, Thomas - E Company/Rgt., Baltimore, 18 (7/18/48).

Pool, Lewis, Musician - D Company/Bn., Washington, 23 (2/28/47).

Porter, Edward P. - G Company (Light Artillery)/Rgt., Baltimore, 32 (7/13/48).

Posey, John P., 4th Sergeant - F Company/Bn., Baltimore, 27 (5/30/46). Soldier filed for pension from Maryland on 6/13/87, S-14346. Resided at Brightside, Baltimore County until his death in 1894. (L-16)

Powell, George W., 2nd Corporal - C Company/Rgt., Baltimore, 36 (4/30/48)

Poulson, William P., 1st Sergeant - B Company/Bn., Baltimore, 39 (5/30/46). Slightly wounded at the Battle of Monterey on 9/21/46. (D-243)

Pratt, Charles - E Company/Bn., Baltimore. Discharged by surgeon's certificate on 8/7/46. Alias John C. Pratt. Soldier filed for pension from California on 3/20/88, S-18843. (K-38)

Pregg, Josiah - E Company/Bn., Baltimore. Discharged by surgeon's certificate on (8/31/46) at Camargo. Alias Isaiah Prag. Soldier filed for pension from Maryland on 3/15/87, S-9885. Wife, Jane A., filed for pension from Maryland on 6/20/89, W-8134. (K-69)

Preston, John D. - F Company/Bn., Baltimore, 22 (5/30/46). Soldier filed for pension from Virginia on 2/14/87, S-5271. Soldier also served in the U.S. Cavalry between 1855-1864.

Price, George W., Corporal - A Company/Bn., Baltimore, 26 (5/30/47)

Purcell, Charles W., - A Company/Bn., Baltimore, 19 (5/30/47). Later served in G Company (Light Artillery) in the Regiment as a 3rd Sergeant.

Purdon, John, 2nd Sergeant - B Company/Rgt., Washington, 31 (8/17/48). Also served as Master Sergeant on the Regimental Staff. Wife, Susan, filed for pension on 1/11/88, W-5710.

Pyle, Joseph - E Company/Rgt., Baltimore, 28 (7/18/48).

Queen, William - A Company/Bn., Baltimore, 19 (9/46). Discharged by surgeon's certificate at Camargo. Alias John W. Queen. Soldier filed for pension from Missouri on 6/26/88, S-19764. Wife, Fannie A., filed for pension from Missouri on 8/23/1906, W-18482.

Quigley, Edward - B Company/Rgt., Washington, 34 (8/17/48).

Quigley, Robert - E Company/Rgt., Baltimore, 19 (7/18/48). Discharged by order.

Quinlen, Charles - B Company/Bn., Baltimore, 25 (5/30/46).

Ramsay, Alexander - E Company/Bn., Baltimore, Killed in action in the Battle of Monterey on 9/21/46. (D-241)

Ramsey, James - E Company/Rgt., Baltimore. Discharged by surgeon's certificate in Jalapa on 3/14/48.

Randall, Joseph - A Company/Bn., Baltimore, 38 (5/30/47). Wife, Mary F., filed for pension from North Carolina on 8/25/87, W-4625.

Randolph, Edward F. - A Company/Bn., Baltimore, 30 (9/46). Discharged by surgeon's certificate at Camargo. Soldier filed for pension from Pennsylvania on 8/22/87, S-16110.

Rank, Joseph - C Company/Bn., Washington, 39 (2/28/47).

Rapley, William - E Company/Bn., Baltimore, 35 (12/31/46).

Rawlings, James - A Company/Rgt., Washington, 33 (7/24/48).

Rawlings, William - E Company/Rgt., Baltimore. Died at Jalapa on April 8, 1848.

Read, William S., Sgt. Major - Battalion Staff, 36 (5/30/46).

Reaney, Richard W. - A Company/Bn., Baltimore, 33 (5/30/47). Later promoted to Sergeant Major in the Battalion Staff.

Reeder, John T. - H Company/Rgt., Washington, 29 (7/15/48).

Reeder, John - E Company/Rgt., Baltimore, 29 (7/18/48).

Reely, Artemus - G Company (Light Artillery)/Bn., Baltimore, 22 (7/13/48).

Reese, John A. - E Company/Bn., Baltimore, 18 (12/31/46). Soldier filed for pension from Maryland on 6/12/88, S-19645. Wife, Mary H., filed for pension from Maryland on 9/27/1906, W-18509. Resided at 212 Fremont Ave., Baltimore in 1895. (L-18)

MARYLAND AND D.C. VOLUNTEERS IN THE MEXICAN WAR

Reeve, William, 4th Sergeant - A Company/Rgt., Washington, 32 (7/24/48).

Reeves, Hazekiah - H Company/Rgt., Washington, 42 (7/15/48).

Reichter, John - A Company/Rgt., Washington, 26 (7/24/48).

Reilly, James - B Company/Bn., Baltimore, 21 (5/30/46). Soldier filed for pension from Pennsylvania on 2/21/87, S-5415.

Reinlein, John - A Company/Rgt., Washington, 28 (7/24/48).

Reitzell, Jacob - A Company/Bn., Baltimore, 20 (9/46). Discharged by surgeon's certificate at Camargo.

Relsjsand, Jonas W. - B Company/Bn., Baltimore.

Ressing, William - D Company/Rgt., Washington, 25 (2/29/48).

Reyner, Samuel - A Company/Rgt., Washington, 42 Sick at Vera Cruz 11/6/47 to 7/24/48.

Reynolds, Charles A. - F Company/Rgt., Baltimore, 19. Discharged at Jalapa on 2/1/48. Resided at 207 E. North Ave., Baltimore until his death on 3/2/96. (L-18)

Reynolds, James - G Company (Light Artillery)/Rgt., Baltimore, 31 (7/13/48).

Reynolds, Joseph - A Company/Bn., Baltimore, 23 (11/46). Discharged by surgeon's certificate.

Rheim, George, Sergeant - B Company/Rgt., Washington, 26 (8/17/48).

Ria, Andrew J. - Recruit Company/Rgt., Baltimore, 35 (2/29/48). Deserted from Fort McHenry on 6/19/47, apprehended on 3/17/48.

Richardson, John - D Company/Bn., Washington, 35 (2/28/47).

Richardson, Joseph B. - E Company/Bn., Baltimore, 23 (12/31/46). Wife, Francis Ann, filed for pension from Maryland on 9/16/90, W-9307.

Rickmarr, Frederick - A Company/Rgt., Washington, 30's (7/24/48).

Rider, George W. - H Company/Rgt., Baltimore, 21 (7/15/48). Soldier filed for pension from Maryland on 6/23/87, S-14525.

Rider, John W., 1st Sergeant - F Company/Bn., Baltimore, 20 (5/30/46).

Ridley, Dennis - A Company/Bn., Baltimore, 22 (5/30/47).

Riely, Artemus - G Company (Light Artillery)/Rgt., Baltimore, 22 (7/13/48).

Riely, Joseph, Corporal - D Company/Bn., Washington, 22 (2/28/47).

Rigdon, James H. - A Company/Bn., Baltimore, 23 (5/30/47). Soldier filed for pension from Maryland on 3/17/87, S-10001. Wife, Margaret, filed for pension from Maryland on 11/16/1901, W-16432.

Riley, Daniel - E Company/Rgt., Baltimore. Wife, Lydia Ann, filed for pension from Pennsylvania on 3/5/87, W-1776.

Riley, John H. - F Company/Rgt., Baltimore, 20 (7/18/48). Alias John H. Riall. Wife, Ann, filed for pension from Maryland on 4/1/87, W-1793. Died prior to 1879. (L-18)

Riley, William M.S. - E Company/Bn., Baltimore, 38 (12/31/46).

Ring, Frederick B. - A Company/Bn., Baltimore, 22 (5/30/47).

Ritter, Andrew J. - E Company/Bn., Baltimore, 25 (12/31/46). Soldier filed for pension from the District of Columbia on 3/21/87, S-10013. Wife, Eliza J., filed for pension from the District of Columbia on 6/2/90, W-9052.

Roals, Abraham - B Company/Bn., Baltimore, 22 (5/30/46).

Robbins, Patrick - A Company/Rgt., Washington, 40's (7/24/48).

Roberts, John - F Company/Rgt., Baltimore, 26. Died at Puente Nacional, Mexico, on 10/31/47.

Robertson, Henry B. - D Company/Bn., Washington, 19 (2/28/47). Soldier filed for pension from the District of Columbia on 5/18/87, S-13259. Wife, Mary, filed for pension from the District of Columbia on 9/18/1900, W-15792. Soldier also served in G Company, 2nd U.S. Dragoons and later in the Civil War with the M Company, 11th Kansas Volunteer Cavalry.

Robey, William, 4th Corporal - F Company/Bn., Baltimore, 23 (5/30/46).

Robinson, Henry - G Company (Light Artillery)/Rgt., Baltimore, 27 (7/13/48).

Robinson, John K. - E Company/Bn., Baltimore, 21 (12/31/46). Wife, Sarah A., filed for pension from the District of Columbia on 3/23/87, W-1829.

Robinson, Levi H. - D Company/Rgt., Philadelphia, 20 (2/29/48).

Robinson, William H. - B Company/Bn., Baltimore, 28 (5/30/46).

Robinson, William - F Company/Bn., Baltimore, 21 (5/30/46).

Robisson, Samuel O. - F Company/Bn., Baltimore, 20 (5/30/46). Deserted.

Rochester, George, 1st Corporal - F Company/Bn., Baltimore, 19 (11/46). Discharged by surgeon's certificate at Monterey.

Rodgers, Alexander, Chief Musician - G Company (Light Artillery)/Rgt., Baltimore, 37 (7/13/48).

Rogers, John - F Company/Rgt., Baltimore. Soldier filed for pension from Pennsylvania on 2/20/88, S-18556. Served in G Company, 17th Pennsylvania Infantry Regiment in the Civil War.

Rogers, Seth S. - E Company/Bn., Baltimore, 24 (12/31/46).

Romboltz, John G. - D Company/Rgt., Washington, 35 (2/29/48).

Rose, Robert - F Company/Rgt., Baltimore, 19 (7/18/48).

Rosenburg, Edward - G Company (Light Artillery)/Rgt., Baltimore, 19 (7/13/48).

Ross, Charles C. - E Company/Rgt., Baltimore, 37 (7/18/48).

Rowlett, Edward - B Company/Rgt., Washington, 21. Died at Jalapa on 12/17/47.

Ruddach, Joseph H., 1st Lieutenant - F Company/Bn., Baltimore. Resided at 372 Park Ave., Baltimore until his death on 10/29/84. (L-18).

Rusk, James - F Company/Bn., Baltimore, 21 (5/30/46).

Russell, A.J. - A Company/Bn., Baltimore, 27 (9/46). Discharged by surgeon's certificate at Camargo.

Russell, Andrew S. - H Company/Rgt., Baltimore, 27 (7/15/48). Dishonorably discharged by regimental court martial on 7/1/48.

Russell, Joseph - B Company/Rgt., Washington, 25 (8/17/48).

Salisbury, John - B Company/Rgt., Washington, 30. Died at Jalapa in 1847.

Sandford, Lynas - D Company/Rgt., Washington, 21 (2/29/48).

Scarburg, Joseph - A Company/Bn., Baltimore, 22 (5/30/47).

Scattergood, John G. - H Company/Rgt., Baltimore, 26 (7/15/48).

Schaeffer, Francis B., Captain, Commanding Officer - D Company/Bn., Washington, Joined unit by promotion from company E on 1/6/47. In September, 1847, he became commanding officer of H Company of the Regiment. Soldier filed for pension from the District of Columbia on 4/29/87, S-12032.

Schaeffer, William A. H. 1st Sergeant - A Company/Bn., Baltimore, 27 (5/30/47). Enlisted in B Company in (5/30/46)

Schaffer, Simon - E Company/Rgt., Baltimore.

Schieck, John P. - F Company/Bn., Baltimore, 21 (5/30/46).

Schmidt, Valentine - E Company/Rgt., Baltimore.

Schnebley, Andrew R., 4th Sergeant - G Company (Light Artillery)/Rgt., Baltimore, 24 (7/13/48). Soldier filed for pension from Pennsylvania on 2/10/87, S-5644. Died on June 11, 1913 at Mercersburg, Pennsylvania.

Schnebly, Freeland - B Company/Bn., Baltimore, 18 (5/30/46).

Schneider, George J. Leo - A Company/Rgt., Washington, 40's Sick at Vera Cruz 11/6/47 to 7/24/48.

Schnell, Andrew R., 4th Sergeant - G Company (Light Artillery)/Rgt.

Schnirden, Anton - A Company/Rgt., Washington, 24. Died in the regimental hospital at Jalapa on 1/28/48.

Schoek, Henry - A Company/Bn., Baltimore, 21 (5/30/47).

Schraick, Nicholas - A Company/Rgt., Washington, 38. Died at the National Bridge, Mexico, regimental hospital on 11/3/47.

Schron, Frederick - A Company/Rgt., Washington, 20's (7/24/48).

Schulenburg, Henry - A Company/Bn., Baltimore, 33 (5/30/47).

Schwalbe, John P. - A Company/Rgt., Washington.

Scott, James - C Company/Rgt., Baltimore, 30 (4/30/48). Wife, Catherine A., filed for pension from Maryland on 5/16/87, W-3297.

Scott, William A. - F Company/Bn., Baltimore, 24 (5/30/46). Deserted.

Search, Edwin K. - F Company/Bn., Baltimore, 22 (5/30/46).

Seim, Charles J. - F Company/Bn., Baltimore, 26 (5/30/46). Wife, Margaret, filed for pension from Maryland on 5/27/87, W-3533.

Seis, George - see Zais, George

Seizd, Frederick, Corporal - A Company/Rgt., Washington. Died in regimental hospital in Jalapa on 12/30/47.

Sesselman, John - C Company/Rgt., Baltimore, 28 (4/30/48). Wife, Barbara, filed for pension from Bavaria on 2/7/91, W-9635.

Sevan, Osborn C. - G Company (Light Artillery)/Rgt.

Severe, Francis F. - H Company/Rgt., Washington, 22 (7/15/48). Soldier filed for pension from Pennsylvania on 9/18/88, S-20325. Soldier also served in C Company, 191st Pennsylvania Infantry Regiment during the Civil War.

Shaefer, Henry - B Company/Rgt., Washington, 31 (8/17/48).

Shanaman, John - F Company/Rgt. Wife, Margaret, filed for pension from Maryland on 7/28/87, W-4338.

Sharion, Patrick - F Company/Rgt., Baltimore, 18 (7/18/48).

Sharkey, John - G Company (Light Artillery)/Rgt.

Shaw, William C. - C Company/Rgt., Baltimore, 31 (4/30/48).

Shillinburg, Henry - A Company/Bn.

Shillonn, Joseph P. - F Company/Bn., Baltimore, 25 (5/30/46).

Shimp, George W. - F Company/Rgt., Baltimore, 18 (7/18/48). Soldier filed for pension from Maryland on 2/5/87, S-5658. Wife, Anna G., filed for pension from Maryland on 11/21/96, W-13637.

Shivers, Robert C. - H Company/Rgt. Wife named Sarah R. Soldier also served in K and M Companies of the 1st Maryland Cavalry Regiment and 13th Pennsylvania Infantry Regiment.

Shmidt, John T. - B Company/Bn., Baltimore, 35 (5/30/46).

Shock, Edward - A Company/Bn.

Shoek, Samuel - F Company/Rgt., Baltimore, 20. Died at Vera Cruz in 2/48.

Short, Isaac - G Company (Light Artillery)/Rgt., Baltimore, 22 (7/13/48).

Shorter, George - B Company/Rgt., Baltimore, 31 (8/17/48).

Shott, George T. - D Company/Bn. Soldier filed for pension from Pennsylvania on 9/7/89, S-22048. Wife, Margaret, filed for pension from Pennsylvania on 10/11/1902, W-16821.

Shula, John J. - C Company/Rgt., Baltimore, 34 (4/30/48).

Shultz, Zachariah, Corporal - B Company/Bn., Baltimore, 22 (5/30/46)

Shwartz, Augustus - H Company/Rgt., Baltimore, 28 (7/15/48). Wife, Lydia, filed for pension from the District of Columbia on 8/23/88, W-7054.

Sibley, William Henson - E Company/Bn., Baltimore, 19 (12/31/46). Soldier filed for pension from the District of Columbia on 2/4/87, S-5126. Wife, Phebe, filed for pension from the District of Columbia on 8/15/93, W-11541.

Simpsoe, William - B Company/Bn., Baltimore, 35 (5/30/46).

Simpson, C.D. - G Company (Light Artillery)/Rgt., Baltimore.

Simpson, Ezeikiel - G Company (Light Artillery)/Rgt., Baltimore, 20 (7/13/48).

Simpson, John F. - D Company/Bn., Washington, 21 (2/28/47). Soldier filed for pension from the District of Columbia on 6/14/87, S-14141.

Simpson, Thomas - A Company/Bn., Baltimore, 22 (5/30/47).

Sinners, Elizah N. - H Company/Rgt., Baltimore, 44 (7/15/48).

Sinton, Thomas J. - E Company/Rgt., Baltimore, 26 (7/18/48), Sick in hospital at Vera Cruz in November, 1847.

Slayton, William - G Company (Light Artillery)/Rgt., Baltimore, 32. Deserted from Fort McHenry on 9/9/47.

Slear, Christopher - C Company/Rgt., Baltimore, 25 (4/30/48).

Sliker, Samuel - E Company/Rgt., Baltimore. Died at Jalapa.

Sloan, William H., Musician - D Company/Rgt., Washington, 28 (2/29/48). Wife, Lucy, filed for pension from the District of Columbia on 4/12/87, W-2625. Bounty Land Warrant #26,336-160-47. Soldier died on March 2, 1858.

Slount, Winslow - B Company/Rgt., Washington, 28 (7/17/48).

Small, James - F Company/Bn., Baltimore, 19 (5/30/46).

Smith, Alexander - A Company/Bn., Baltimore, 20 (5/30/47).

Smith, Alexander N. - C Company/Rgt., Baltimore, 34 (4/30/48).

Smith, Charles - A Company/Bn., Baltimore, 19 (5/30/47).

Smith, Francis F. - Recruit Company/Rgt., Baltimore, 19 (2/29/48). Alias Frank. Soldier filed for pension from Maryland on 4/18/88, S-19155. Wife, Elizabeth S., filed for pension from Maryland on 4/12/1902.

Smith, Frederick - A Company/Rgt., Baltimore, 34 (7/24/48).

Smith, Hugh - F Company/Rgt., Baltimore, 20 (7/18/48). Wife, Mary V., filed for pension from Virginia on 7/7/88, W-6825.

Smith, John - E Company/Bn., Baltimore, 34. Deserted at camp near Monterey on 12/12/46.

Smith, John M., 2nd Sergeant - B Company/Bn., Baltimore, 22 (5/30/46). Died prior to 1879. (L-19)

Smith, John B. - F Company/Bn., Baltimore, 34 (5/30/46). Deserted.

Smith, Robert - F Company/Rgt., Baltimore, 18. Discharged by surgeon's certificate at Puente Nacional, Mexico, on 9/24/47.

Smith, Samuel E., 3rd Lieutenant - F Company/Bn., Baltimore. (B-7/21/46-1)

Smith, Y.J.W., 2nd Sergeant - E Company/Rgt., Baltimore, 22 (7/18/48). Soldier filed for pension from Maryland on 10/24/87, S-17158.

Snowden, Marcellus E. - A Company/Bn., Baltimore, 23 (9/46). Discharged by surgeon's certificate at Camargo. Soldier filed for pension from Ohio on 8/2/87, S-6050.

Snyder, John A. - H Company/Rgt., Baltimore, 31 (7/15/48).

Spalding, George - D Company/Rgt., Washington, 21. Discharged by surgeon's certificate at Jalapa on 2/23/48. Soldier filed for pension from Maryland on 4/12/87, S-10293.

Spillman, Joshua - A Company/Bn., Baltimore, 20 (5/30/47). Wife, Francis E., filed for pension from Georgia on 9/25/93, W-11020.

Sprigg, William - C Company/Bn., Washington, 18 (2/28/47).

Stansbury, Edward H. - H Company/Rgt., Baltimore, 21 (7/15/48). Soldier filed for pension from Maryland on 6/27/88, S-19769. Wife, Ann R., filed for pension from Maryland on 8/14/90, W-9224.

Stansbury, Thomas T. - E Company/Bn., Baltimore, 23 (12/31/46).

Stayton, William - Recruit Company/Rgt., Baltimore, 32. Discharged by surgeon's certificate from Fort McHenry on 3/26/48.

Stedrens, William R. - F Company/Rgt., Baltimore, 25. Died in Mexico on 4/10/48.

Steel, James, 2nd Lieutenant - F Company/Rgt., Baltimore, Also served as adjutant for the Regiment. Wife, Mattie E., filed for pension from California on 4/23/88, W-6366.

Steele, William - see Giffen, Robert.

Stephens, Thomas W. - H Company/Rgt., Washington, 25 (7/15/48).

Stephenson, Edward W., 2nd Corporal - F Company/Bn., Baltimore, 20 (5/30/46).

Stettinius, J.W.H., Assistant Surgeon - Battalion Staff, Washington, Son of Samuel Stettinius of Washington. (B-9/19/46-1)

Steuart, Charles B. - F Company/Bn., Baltimore, 21 (5/30/46). Soldier filed for pension from Maryland on 2/4/87, S-6152.

Steuart, James A., Commanding Officer, Captain - A Company/Bn., Baltimore.

Stevens, John - B Company/Bn., Baltimore, 26 (5/30/46). Died on 8/19/46. (B-10/16/46-1)

Stevenson, E.W. - F Company/Bn., Baltimore, Slightly wounded at the Battle of Monterey on 9/21/46. (D-243)

Stevenson, John - D Company/Bn., Washington, 21 (2/28/47).

Steward, George - C Company/Bn., Washington, 20 (2/28/47).

Stewart, John - F Company/Rgt., Baltimore, 20 (7/18/48).

Stewart, John N. - F Company/Rgt., Baltimore, 20 (7/18/48).

Stewart, William N., 3rd Sergeant - F Company/Rgt., Baltimore, 33 (7/18/48).

Stiff, William F., Corporal - B Company/Bn., Baltimore, 21 (5/30/46). Wife, Mary A., filed for pension from Pennsylvania on 1/31/93, W-11100.

Stinchcomb, John D. - A Company/Bn., Baltimore, 20 (5/30/47). Died on 2/1/84. (L-19)

Stinchcomb, Noah W. - D Company/Bn., Washington. Discharged by surgeon's certificate at Monterey 1/14/47. Soldier filed for pension from Illinois on 3/21/87, S-10352. Died on 1/1/1916 in Edwardsville, Illinois. Also served in the Civil War with the 150th Illinois Infantry Regiment.

Stiner, Daniel - C Company/Bn., Washington, 19 (1/14/47). Discharged by surgeon's certificate at Monterey.

Stits, William - F Company/Rgt., Baltimore, 25 (7/18/48).

Stockbarger, John W. - D Company/Rgt. Soldier filed for pension from Oregon on 5/3/88, S-19295.

Stockton, Lewis F., Corporal - C Company/Bn., Washington, 38 (2/28/47)

Stone, Melvin J. or S. - F Company/Bn., Baltimore, 22 (5/30/46). Slightly wounded at the Battle of Monterey on 9/21/46. Soldier filed for pension from Ohio on 3/2/87, S-6238. (D-243)

Storm, John - C Company/Bn., Washington, 22 (1/14/47). Discharged by surgeon's certificate at Monterey.

Stout, Frances - E Company/Rgt., Baltimore.

Strahm, Christian - H Company/Rgt. Soldier filed for pension from Idaho on 3/3/87, S-6247. Wife, Mary J., filed for pension from Idaho on 4/8/1907, W-18666.

Stroft, Michial, Corporal - B Company/Bn., Baltimore,

Stump, Frederick - B Company/Bn., Baltimore, 32 (5/30/46).

Stump, James - G Company (Light Artillery)/Rgt. Soldier filed for pension from the District of Columbia on 10/18/87, S-17079.

Sullivan, James W. - E Company/Bn., Baltimore, 23 (12/31/46).

Summers, George - F Company/Bn., Baltimore, 20 (5/30/46).

Sunderland, Henry - A Company/Bn., Baltimore, 25 (5/30/47).

Surghnor, Thompson - G Company (Light Artillery)/Rgt., Baltimore, 30's (7/13/48). Wife, Martha, filed for pension from West Virginia on 7/2/87, W-3618.

Swaits, Joseph - C Company/Rgt., Camp Berggara, Mexico, 35 (4/30/48).

Swan, George E. - C Company/Rgt., Baltimore, 19 (4/30/48).

Swan, Oswald C. - G Company (Light Artillery)/Rgt., Baltimore, 23 (7/13/48). Soldier filed for pension from Missouri on 4/27/87, S-12079.

Swift, Charles B., 4th Corporal - G Company (Light Artillery)/Rgt., Baltimore, 22 (7/13/48). Wife, Henrietta, filed for pension from Kentucky on 6/4/87, W-3619.

Swineburger, Christopher - B Company/Rgt., Baltimore, 31 (8/17/48).

Talbot, George - H Company/Rgt., Baltimore, 21 (7/15/48).

Talbot, Jeremiah - C Company/Rgt., Baltimore, 19 (4/30/48). Soldier filed for pension from Virginia on 7/24/89, S-21910.

Talbott, Nicholas B. - F Company/Rgt., Baltimore, 18 (7/18/48). Resided at 1635 E. Fayette St., Baltimore until his death on 3/25/92. Soldier filed for pension from Maryland on 7/21/87, S-15304. Wife, Mary A., filed for pension from Maryland on 2/8/93, no number provided. Served in H Company of the 5th Maryland Infantry Regiment during the Civil War. Held the rank of 2nd Lieutenant. (L-20) (P-210)

Talbot, William A. - A Company/Bn., Baltimore, 21 (5/30/47).

Taney, Joseph - F Company/Rgt., Baltimore, 21 (7/18/48). Wife, Mary V., filed for pension from Maryland on 3/4/87, W-2122.

Taneyhill, James, 3rd Lieutenant - F Company/Bn., Baltimore, 25 (5/30/46). Died of wounds at Rio Calaboso on 7/25/47. (H-672)

Tarring, James - A Company/Bn., Baltimore, 24 (5/30/47).

Tavenner, George - see Ball, George

Taylor, John - D Company/Bn., Washington, 22 (2/28/47).

Taylor, Marcellus, K., 1st Lieutenant - B Company/Bn., Baltimore, Also served as Captain and commanding officer of F Company in the Regiment.

Taylor, Samuel - D Company/Rgt., Washington, 23 (2/29/48).

Taylor, William - G Company (Light Artillery)/Rgt., Baltimore, 36 (7/13/48). Resided at 225 S. Calhoun Street, Baltimore in 1895. (L-20)

Tellinga, E.W. - F Company/Rgt., Jalapa, Mexico, 40's (7/18/48).

Tensfield, Arnold, 2nd Lieutenant - G Company (Light Artillery)/Rgt., Baltimore, 32 (7/13/48). Acting ordnance officer at Jalapa.

Tensfield, John, Artificer - G Company (Light Artillery)/Rgt., Baltimore, 39 (7/13/48). Died on 6/2/87. Daughter, Mrs. E. Carville of Kent Island, Queen Anne's County, Maryland, wrote John Kenly concerning application for pension following his death. (R-507)

Thayre, Stephen - Recruit Company/Rgt., Baltimore, 17 (4/30/48).

Thomas, George H. - F Company/Bn., Baltimore, 21 (5/30/46). Soldier filed for pension from Iowa on 5/10/87, S-12834.

Thomas, William - D Company/Bn., Washington, 23 (2/28/47).

MARYLAND AND D.C. VOLUNTEERS IN THE MEXICAN WAR

Thompson, Alexander - F Company/Rgt., Baltimore, 25 (7/18/48). Soldier filed for pension from Maryland on 5/29/88, S-19521. Also served in the Civil War as a private in H Company, 11th Maryland Infantry Regiment, between 6/11/64 and 10/1/64. (P-389)

Thompson, Benjamin T. - B Company/Rgt., Washington, 31. Discharged by surgeon's certificate at Fort McHenry on 7/8/47.

Thompson, David H. - H Company/Rgt. Soldier filed for pension from Nevada on 2/26/87, S-6406.

Thompson, Edward, Musician - A Company/Bn., Baltimore, 44 (11/46). Discharged by surgeon's certificate.

Thompson, John H., 1st Sergeant - B Company/Rgt., Washington, 29 (8/17/48). Soldier filed for pension from the District of Columbia on 2/24/87, S-6420. Wife, Phebe E., filed for pension from the District of Columbia on 12/7/96, W-13664.

Thompson, John - G Company (Light Artillery)/Rgt., Baltimore, 19 (7/13/48). Discharged by civil process.

Thornton, John M., 1st Lieutenant - B Company/Rgt., Washington, 30 (8/17/48). Wife, Harriet A., filed for pension from the District of Columbia on 2/11/87, W-2161.

Tibbles, James, Corporal - E Company/Bn., Baltimore. Discharged by surgeon's certificate on (8/31/46) at Camargo. (K-69)

Tierney, James - E Company/Rgt., Baltimore. Deserted from Fort McHenry in the summer of 1847.

Tilghman, Frisbie, 1st Lieutenant - G Company (Light Artillery)/Rgt., Baltimore, 35 (7/13/48). Resigned 5/16/48.

Tilghman, Lloyd, Captain, Commanding Officer - G Company (Light Artillery)/Rgt., Baltimore, 30 (7/13/48). Later served in the Confederate Army during the Civil War as a Brigadier General. He was killed in action at the Battle of Baker's Creek, Mississippi on 5/16/1863.

Tilghman, Stedman R., Surgeon of the Regiment. Died of sickness at New Orleans on 6/28/48. (K-281)

Tissfrits, Samuel - B Company/Rgt., Washington, 23. Died at Jalapa on 1/4/48.

Titlow, John - G Company (Light Artillery)/Rgt., Baltimore, 26 (7/13/48).

Todd, George W., 1st Corporal - F Company/Rgt., Baltimore, 24 (7/18/48).

Tolbert, John - G Company (Light Artillery)/Rgt., Baltimore, 20's (7/13/48).

Tolson, Douglas - D Company/Bn., Washington, 20 (2/28/47). Wife, Rebecca, filed for pension from the District of Columbia on 2/11/87, W-2174.

Toole, Henry - C Company/Rgt., Baltimore, 45. Discharged by surgeon's certificate at Jalapa on 3/14/48.

Tracey, Hugh - A Company/Bn., Baltimore, 21 (5/30/47).

Traverse, Tolerance J. - C Company/Rgt., Baltimore, 24 (4/30/48).

Traynor, James - G Company (Light Artillery)/Rgt., Baltimore, 30's (7/13/48).

Trescart, John, 1st Sergeant - B Company/Bn., Baltimore, Killed in action at the Battle of Monterey on 9/21/46. (D-241)

Tressel, Ernest - E Company/Bn., Baltimore. Discharged by surgeon's certificate on (8/31/46) at Camargo. (K-69)

Trippard, James B. - H Company/Rgt., Baltimore, 18 (7/15/48).

Troxall, David M. - G Company (Light Artillery)/Rgt., Baltimore, 21 Deserted from Fort McHenry on 8/15/47.

Tucker, Charles H. - A Company/Rgt., Washington, 19 (7/24/48).

Tucker, William W., 3rd Sergeant - D Company/Rgt., Washington, 24. Discharged by surgeon's certificate from general hospital at Vera Cruz in 12/47.

Turner, George A. - G Company (Light Artillery)/Rgt., Baltimore, 23 Deserted from Fort McHenry on 8/27/47.

Turner, John W. - E Company/Bn., Baltimore. Discharged by surgeon's certificate on 8/7/46. Soldier filed for pension from Maryland on 8/5/87, S-15691. (K-38)

Turner, Joshua - Recruit Company/Rgt., Baltimore, 21 (4/30/48).

Turner, Robert - E Company/Rgt., Baltimore, 28 (7/18/48). Listed as a deserter, later appears on rolls of H Company of the Regiment.

Tuthill, David M. - F Company/Bn., Baltimore, 21 (5/30/46).

Tuttle, Charles - F Company/Bn., Baltimore, 24 (5/30/46). Died prior to 1879. Wife, Rebecca Jane, filed for pension from Maryland on 2/12/87, W-2202. (L-20)

Tyler, George - C Company/Bn., Washington, 39 (2/28/47).

Tyser, Thomas, Sergeant - E Company/Bn., Baltimore, 23 (12/31/46).

Vail, Rowen - C Company/Bn., Washington, Transferred to company C on 1/16/47.

Van Horn, Albert - Recruit Company/Rgt., Baltimore, 23. Discharged by civil process on 3/30/48.

Verlandies, William - Recruit Company/Rgt., Baltimore, 23. Deserted from Fort McHenry on 3/15/48, apprehended on 3/20/48. Deserted again on 3/21/48.

Vermillion, Charles - D Company/Bn., Washington, 19 (2/28/47). Soldier filed for pension from the District of Columbia on 2/4/87, S-6618. Wife, Elizabeth, filed for pension from the District of Columbia on 2/20/95, W-12572.

Vernon, Patrick - G Company (Light Artillery)/Rgt., Baltimore, 30's (7/13/48).

Vernon, William - F Company/Bn., Baltimore, 18 (5/30/46).

Vogle, Valentine - A Company/Rgt., Washington, 20's (7/24/48).

Volandt, William - G Company (Light Artillery)/Rgt., Baltimore, 24. Deserted from Fort McHenry on 9/5/47. Discharged on 4/7/48.

Waffers, Jacob, 4th Sergeant - B Company/Rgt., Washington, 25 (8/17/48).

Wagner, George W., Sergeant - A Company/Bn., Baltimore, 28 (5/30/47). Wife, Rosa, filed for pension from Maryland on 8/13/91, W-10037.

Wagner, Henry - E Company/Rgt., Baltimore. Died in Vera Cruz.

Wagner, James (or Joseph?) E. - F Company/Bn., Baltimore, 22 (5/30/46). Soldier filed for pension from Maryland on 2/23/87, S-6659.

Walden, James - H Company/Rgt., Baltimore, 26 (7/15/48).

Walker, James D. - D Company/Rgt., Baltimore, 36 (2/29/48).

Walker, John S. - A Company/Bn., Baltimore, 22 (5/26/47). Died in hospital 5/26/47.

Walker, Robert L. - E Company/Rgt., Baltimore. Deserted from Fort McHenry in the summer of 1847.

Wallace, Patrick - G Company (Light Artillery)/Rgt., Baltimore, 22. Deserted from Fort McHenry on 9/4/47.

Wallack, Robert - H Company/Rgt., Baltimore, 20 (7/15/48).

Waller, Edward L., Sergeant - B Company/Rgt., Washington, 24 (8/17/48). Wife, Elizabeth A., filed for pension from the District of Columbia on 8/29/87, W-4667. Soldier also served in A Company, 4th U.S. Artillery between 1868-1871. Served in the 1st District of Columbia Volunteer Infantry Regiment during the Civil War.

Walsh, James - G Company (Light Artillery)/Rgt., Baltimore, 38 (7/13/48).

Walter, George - A Company/Bn., Baltimore, 26 (5/30/47).

Walter, Henry - A Company/Bn., Baltimore, 23 (5/30/47). Resided in Clinton, Baltimore County in 1894. Soldier filed for pension from Maryland on 2/24/87, S-6716. Wife, Maggie J., filed for pension from Maryland on 7/9/1908, W-19079. (L-22)

Ward, Daniel - E Company/Rgt., Baltimore, 20 (7/18/48).

Warick, Abner - Recruit Company/Rgt., Baltimore, 24. Deserted from Fort McHenry on 3/12/48, apprehended on 3/20/48. Deserted again on 3/21/48.

Warren, William F. - G Company (Light Artillery)/Rgt., Baltimore.

Warrington, Stephen H. - A Company/Bn., Baltimore, 19 (5/30/47). Soldier filed for pension from the District of Columbia on 12/4/88, S-20820. Wife, Mary B., filed for pension from the District of Columbia on 2/9/1900, W-15479.

Waters, John, Captain - Commanding Officer, D Company/Bn., Washington, Resigned 11/23/46. In 1846, he was market master and constable, residing on the west side of West 10th Street, between G and H Streets north. (W-1846).

Waters, Peter L. - G Company (Light Artillery)/Rgt., Baltimore, 30's (7/13/48).

Watkins, Nicholas - A Company/Rgt., Washington, 20's (7/24/48).

Watson, Justice - D Company/Rgt., Philadelphia, 20 (2/29/48).

Watson, William H., Lieutenant Colonel, Commanding Officer of the Battalion. He was born on August 30, 1808 in Baltimore City. After being educated in the City, he passed the Baltimore County Bar on January 14, 1829 and entered the law practice of his uncle, Colonel William H. Freeman. He later served as a magistrate and in 1836 was elected to the city council. By 1838, Watson was serving as Baltimore's representative in the House of Delegates and in his second term was granted the speakership of the House. Watson maintained an interest in the military which resulted in his joining a militia organization (the Independent Blues) in the state. Governor

Pratt of Maryland in 1845 appointed him a colonel on the military staff of the Governor. Also at this time, he continued his practice as an attorney in Baltimore at number 8 Courthouse Lane while residing at 164 E. Pratt Street. Killed in action in the Battle of Monterey on 9/21/46. Buried at Greenmount Cemetery in Baltimore. (C-1845) (D-240) (M-887).

Watson, William H. - A Company/Bn., Baltimore, 20 (5/30/47).

Watton, Robert N., Corporal - B Company/Bn., Baltimore, 22 (5/30/46)

Watts, James - B Company/Rgt., Washington, 30 (8/17/48).

Wayson, James - F Company/Rgt., Baltimore, 21 (7/18/48).

Weaver, John - E Company/Rgt., Baltimore, 26 (7/18/48).

Webb, Daniel C. - F Company/Rgt., Baltimore, 35 (7/18/48).

Webber, Alexander - F Company/Rgt., Baltimore, 22. Discharged at Jalapa on 2/1/48. Soldier filed for pension from Maryland on 8/30/87, S-16253.

Webster, Henry W. - G Company (Light Artillery)/Rgt., Baltimore, 31 (7/13/48). Resided at 106 West Barre St., Baltimore until his death on 8/28/94. Soldier filed for pension from Maryland on 4/19/89, S-21543. Wife, Elizabeth P.H., filed for pension from Maryland on 10/4/94, W-12345. (L-22)

Webster, Joshua W. - F Company/Rgt., Baltimore, 18 (7/18/48). Soldier filed for pension from Virginia on 2/26/87, S-6806. Wife, Isabella T., filed for pension from Maryland on 10/28/96, W-13609.

Weeks, William H. - D Company/Bn., Washington, 28 (2/28/47). Soldier filed for pension from New York on 5/21/87, S-13290.

Weeks, William H. - F Company/Bn., Baltimore, 23 (5/30/46).

Weems, William M. - G Company (Light Artillery)/Rgt., Baltimore. Wife, Mary J., filed for pension from the District of Columbia on 5/12/93, W-11355.

Wegner, Henry - A Company/Rgt., Washington, 36 Sick at Vera Cruz 11/6/47 to 7/24/48.

Weiland, George C. - D Company/Rgt., Baltimore, 24 (2/29/48).

Welch, Ephraim - C Company/Rgt., Baltimore, 18 (4/30/48).

Welch (or Welsh), James - F Company/Rgt., Baltimore, 20 (7/18/48). Soldier filed for pension from Pennsylvania on 3/17/87, S-10634.

Welch, John B., 3rd Corporal - A Company/Bn., Baltimore, 29 (5/30/47). Also served in the E Company/Rgt.

Wells, Daniel - F Company/Bn., Baltimore, 19 (5/30/46).

Wells, John - D Company. Soldier filed for pension from the District of Columbia on 5/9/87, S-12887. Wife, Mary J., filed for pension from the District of Columbia on 3/20/1908, W-18963.

Welsh, James - B Company/Bn., Baltimore, 18 (5/30/46).

Wenholz, Frederick - C Company/Rgt., Baltimore, 25 (4/30/48). Soldier filed for pension from Pennsylvania on 2/10/87, S-6865. Wife, Eleanore Emilie, filed for pension from Pennsylvania on 10/31/1901, W-16413.

West, Benjamin R., 2nd Lieutenant - D Company/Rgt., Washington, 27 (2/29/48).

West, James W. - C Company/Rgt., Baltimore, 32 (4/30/48).

Wharry, Joseph - E Company/Bn., Baltimore.

Wheeden, D.B. - A Company/Bn., Baltimore, 18 (5/18/46). Deserted.

Wheeler, Nathaniel - C Company/Rgt., Baltimore, 24 (4/30/48).

Whitcomb, Otis Jr., Corporal - F Company/Bn., Baltimore, 23 (5/30/46).

White, Charles, Sergeant - B Company/Rgt., Baltimore, 32. Died at Vera Cruz on 11/11/47.

White, George W. - F Company/Bn., Baltimore, 21 (5/30/46).

White, John P., 4th Corporal - C Company/Bn., Washington, Elected Corporal in Washington City. (N-5/20/46-1)

Whitney, Charles - B Company/Rgt., Washington, 43 (7/17/48). Discharged by surgeon's certificate at New Orleans on 2/4/48.

Wicker, Jacob - F Company/Bn., Baltimore, 25 (5/30/46). Resident of Baltimore, died on 8/19/46. (B-10/16/46)

Widmer, Jacob - F Company/Rgt., Baltimore, 21. Discharged at Jalapa on 1/1/48.

Wilby, Charles C., 1st Corporal - G Company (Light Artillery)/Rgt., Baltimore, 32 (7/13/48).

Wild, Thomas, Corporal - C Company/Bn., Washington, 39 (2/28/47).

Willard, Daniel - F Company/Rgt., Baltimore, 43 (7/18/48).

Willett, Francis - B Company/Rgt., Washington, 29. Discharged by surgeon's certificate at Vera Cruz on 2/10/48. Soldier filed for pension from Maryland on 2/7/87, S-7048. Wife, Margaret A., filed for pension from Maryland on 11/16/96, W-13628. Also bounty land warrant #12,201-160-47.

Williams, Andrew J. - A Company/Bn., Baltimore, 20 (5/30/47). Reported to be sick at San Luis. Soldier filed for pension from the District of Columbia on 4/6/89, S-21492. Wife, Martha A., filed for pension from the District of Columbia on 8/25/98, W-14708. (B-5/24/47-1)

Williams, Daniel W. - E Company/Bn., Baltimore, 19 (12/31/46). Soldier filed for pension from Indiana on 1/13/88, S-18227.

Williams, Henry - G Company (Light Artillery)/Rgt., Baltimore. Discharged by civil process.

Wills, John - D Company/Bn., Washington, 22 (2/28/47).

Wilson, James - F Company/Bn., Baltimore, 22 (5/30/46).

Wilson, John - G Company (Light Artillery)/Rgt., Baltimore, 21 (7/13/48).

Wilson, Johnson - B Company/Bn., Baltimore, 33 (5/30/46).

Wilson, Joseph W. - F Company/Rgt., Baltimore, 28 (7/18/48).

Wilson, Lancelot - D Company/Rgt., Washington, 38. Died in general hospital at Jalapa on 1/22/48.

Wilson, Robert - C Company/Rgt., Baltimore, 21 (4/30/48).

Wilson, Thomas - F Company/Rgt., Baltimore, 20 (7/18/48).

Wilson, William C. - E Company/Bn., Baltimore. Discharged by surgeon's certificate on 8/31/46 at Camargo. Soldier filed for pension from Pennsylvania on 2/11/88, S-7108. Wife, Louisa, filed for pension from Pennsylvania on 11/17/91, W-10223. (K-69)

Wilson, William H., 2nd Corporal - E Company/Rgt., Baltimore, 27 (7/18/48). Soldier filed for pension from New York on 2/21/88, S-18629. Wife, Sarah J., filed for pension from New York on 7/9/94, W-12200.

Wilt, Samuel, 2nd Lieutenant - A Company/Bn., Baltimore.

Wilters, James - D Company/Rgt., Baltimore, 24 (2/29/48).

Wingate, Thomas J. - F Company/Bn., Baltimore, 18 (5/30/46). Also served in H Company of the Regiment.

Wingate, William H. - E Company/Rgt., Baltimore, 19 (7/18/48).

COMPENDIUM OF VOLUNTEERS 77

Witney, Charles

Wolf, Louis - F Company/Bn., Baltimore, 19 (5/30/46).

Wolf, Samuel - B Company/Rgt., Washington, 30. Discharged by surgeon's certificate at Vera Cruz on 2/5/48.

Wolfe, George - E Company/Rgt., Baltimore, 28 (7/18/48). Soldier filed for pension from Maryland on 5/9/87, S-12926. Wife, Araminta L., filed for pension from Maryland on 6/21/88, W-6746.

Wolfe, John - B Company/Bn., Baltimore, 34 (5/30/46). Buried in Mexico on 1/18/47. (A-MS-1902)

Wood, Andrew J. - G Company (Light Artillery)/Rgt., Baltimore, 34 (7/13/48). Soldier filed for pension from Ohio on 3/3/87, S-7185. Wife, Margaret A., filed for pension from Ohio on 5/1/99, W-15075.

Wood, John - F Company/Bn., Baltimore, 23 (5/30/46). Soldier filed for pension from the District of Columbia on 3/2/87, S-7193. Wife, Elizabeth, filed for pension from the District of Columbia on 4/27/90, W-8937.

Wood, Thomas W. - D Company/Rgt., Washington, 23 (2/29/48).

Wood, William H. - F Company/Bn., Baltimore, 21 (5/30/46). Also served as 4th Sergeant in the H Company of the Regiment. Resided at Owings Mill, Maryland until his death on 3/1/80. (L-22)

Woodfield, Joseph, Musician - C Company/Bn., Washington, 26 (2/28/47). Wife, Kazia, filed for pension from Maryland on 6/10/87, W-3674.

Woods, Charles S. - A Company/Bn., Baltimore, 23 (5/30/47).

Woods, William H., 4th Sergeant

Woodward, Henry P. - H Company/Rgt., Baltimore, 21 (7/15/48).

Woodward, William A. - C Company/Bn., Washington, 27 (2/28/47). Elected 4th Sergeant in Washington City. (N-5/20/46-1)

Worrell, William - F Company/Bn., Baltimore, 21 (5/30/46). Deserted.

Worry, Joseph - E Company/Bn., Baltimore, Killed in action at the Battle of Monterey on 9/21/46. (D-241)

Wright, John H. - B Company/Bn., Baltimore, 18 (5/30/46).

Wright, John W., 1st Sergeant - F Company/Rgt., Baltimore, 23 (7/18/48). Soldier filed for pension from Maryland on 7/22/87, S-15344. Wife, Mary E., filed for pension from Maryland on 1/24/99, W-14908.

Wright, Joshua - C Company/Rgt., Baltimore, 25 (4/30/48). Mary Ann Crowther, formerly Mary Ann Wright (Loudenslager, maiden name), mother of soldier, wrote John Kenly concerning pension after son's death. (R-507)

Wyman, Henry - G Company (Light Artillery)/Rgt., Baltimore.

Yeck, Charles - D Company/Bn., Washington, 27 (2/28/47). Wife, Louisa L., filed for pension from Illinois on 2/14/87, W-2388.

Yeitman, John - C Company/Rgt., Baltimore, 24 (4/30/48).

Young, ?. H. - G Company (Light Artillery)/Rgt., Baltimore. Deserted from Fort McHenry on 9/11/47.

Young, Benjamin - D Company/Rgt., Baltimore, 23 (6/24/47).

Young, N. - B Company/Rgt., Washington, 21 (8/17/48).

Young, Thomas, Musician - B Company/Rgt., Washington, 30 (8/17/48).

Young, William - F Company/Bn., Baltimore, 28 (5/30/46).

Young, William - G Company (Light Artillery)/Rgt., Baltimore, 23. Deserted from Fort McHenry on 9/11/47.

Zais, George - G Company/Rgt. Alias George Seis. Wife, Mary A., filed for pension from Maryland on 10/28/87, W-5210.

Zell, Jacob - B Company/Bn., Baltimore, 19 (5/30/46). Soldier filed for pension from Tennessee on 2/16/91, S-23353. Wife, Louisa, filed for pension from Tennessee on 1/3/95, W-12496.

MUSTER ROLL FOR THE BALTIMORE AND
DISTRICT OF COLUMBIA VOLUNTEERS BATTALION

Watson's Battalion Staff

Watson, William H., Commanding Officer, Lt. Col.
Buchanan, Robert C., Commander of Staff, Brevet Major
Aisquith, William E., Adjutant, Brevet 2nd Lieutenant
Shaffer, Francis B., Adjutant
Miles, Smythe M., Surgeon

Lennox, William T., Sgt. Major
Hyde, William S., Sgt. Major
Reaney, R. W., Sgt. Major
Day, Alfred, Sgt. Major
Hooper, John, 2nd M. Sgt.
Read, William S., Sgt. Major

Company A: Baltimore and District of Columbia Volunteers Battalion

Steuart, James A., Commanding Officer, Captain
Bowie, F. Owen, 1st Lieutenant
Wilt, Samuel, 2nd Lieutenant
Chapman, David T., Brevet 2nd Lieutenant

Schaeffer, William A. H. 1st Sergeant
Claypool, William, Sergeant
Wagner, George W., Sergeant
Freeburger, George A., Sergeant
Hyde, William S., Sergeant

Albright, John S. 1st Corporal
Price, George W., Corporal
Messick, James, Corporal
Keller, Jesse, Corporal

Privates

Armstrong, James
Aley, John
Baxley, James
Balderson, William S.
Brown, James
Bowers, George
Briceland, Benjamin
Butler, George
Carr, William M.
Clayrole, William
Donnely, Robert S.
Degant, Joseph
Edwards, John J.
Flynn, Thomas
Ferney, John S.
Fay, William
Frost, James
Gosnell, Joshua
Gosnell, Enoch
Giffen, Robert
Gould, Charles W.
Gray, John T.
Gray, Benjamin F.
Hye, Ezekiell
Hunter, William S.
Howard, Charles B.
Hale, Caleb
Hilt, John R.
Jones, William H.
Jones, Walter
Klockgether, William

Keller, Jesse
Kuhnes, Joseph
Lee, William
Love, Samuel C.
Morgan, John
Moran, John
Major, James C.
Purcell, Charles
Phelps, William
Ridley, Dennis
Reaney, Richard W.
Rigdon, James H.
Ring, Frederick B.
Schoek, Henry
Randall, Joseph
Scarburg, Joseph
Sunderland, Henry
Stinchcomb, John
Schulenburg, Henry
Simpson, Thomas
Smith, Charles
Smith, Alexander
Spillman, Joshua
Tracey, Hugh
Talbot, William A.
Tarring, James
Williams, Andrew J.
Walker, John S.
Walter, George
Warrington, Stephen
Walter, Henry
Watson, William H.

Welsh, John B.
Woods, Charles S.
Lennox, William T.
Hooper, John
Martin, Joseph
McNeil, John W.
Byrne, Thomas
Baxley, George C.
Billington, Gover
Carroll, John W.
Gray, Walter B.
Garrison, Joseph
Snowden, Marcellus E.
Queen, William
Parlette, William A.
Russell, A.J.
Reitzell, Jacob
Merritt, William C.
Randolph, Edward F.
Hart, Albert
Files, Joseph
Lightner, William
Reynolds, Joseph
Thompson, Edward
Hughes, James
Cole, George W.
Childs, George A.
Alexander, William P.
Cassles, Robert M.
Wheeden, D.B.

MARYLAND AND D.C. VOLUNTEERS IN THE MEXICAN WAR

Company B: Baltimore and District of Columbia Volunteers Battalion

Piper, James S., Commanding Officer, Captain

Taylor, Marcellus, K., 1st Lieutenant
Dolan, Lawrence, 2nd Lieutenant
Marrow, Isaac H., Brevet 2nd Lieutenant

Mullen, James, 1st Sergeant
Pouelson, William F., 1st Sergeant
Smith, John M., 2nd Sergeant
Gad, Owen, Sergeant
Chorman, Ernest G., Sergeant
Horseler, Samuel C., Sergeant
Watton, Robert N., Corporal

Nichols, Isaac, Corporal
Stiff, William F., Corporal
Stroft, Michial, Corporal
Kierle, Robert W., Corporal
Shultz, Zachariah, Corporal

Johnson, John B., Musician
Pioneer, William H., Musician

Privates
Anderson, John R.
Armacost, Joshua C.
Althouse, Tobias
Blanchard, Constantine
Bartman, Daniel
Beall, John E.
Bowman, Joseph
Cloomy, John
Curier, Samuel
Clarke, Joshua C.
Copperstone, John
Costello, Henry R.
Cologan, Thomas
Dimmitt, Joshua
Donavan, Jeremiah H.
Faherty, Joseph
Gardiner, John
Gibson, William
Gallager, William
Horan, Timothy
Hearst, Leonard C.
Harrington, Robert
Hanold, George
Kaihart, Joseph

Logan, Alexander
Moran, Owen
Mitchell, Charles
Mitchell, John
Morris, Thomas P.
Morton, William
McCourt, John
McCormick, William
McNeir, Joseph R.
O'Leary, Cornelius
Peterson, William
Quinlen, Charles
Reily, James
Relsjsand, Jonas W.
Schnebly, Freeland
Simpsoe, William
Shmidt, John T.
Wolfe, John
Welsh, James
Kraft, Michael
Beachum, Benjamin
Baker, John
Cooper, John H.
Devyer, Thomas
Day, Alfred

Elliott, James
Garretson, David
Honiser, Alfred
Hurst, Leonard C.
Johnson, James W.
Johnson, John B.
Keirle, Robert W.
Morton, Charles D.
Mullen, James Jr.
Northerman, Henry B.
Nichols, Isaac
O'Brien, Patrick
Perdigue, Francis
Powelson, William F.
Roals, Abraham
Robinson, William H.
Stevens, John
Stiff, William F.
Stump, Frederick
Schaeffer, William
Wright, John H.
Wilson, Johnson
Zell, Jacob

MUSTER ROLL FOR THE BALTIMORE AND D.C. BATTALION

Company C: Baltimore and District of Columbia Volunteers Battalion

Bronaugh, Robert, Captain

Bell, Phineas B., 1st Lieutenant
Gleason, Thomas M., 1st Lieutenant
Hemmick, Jacob C., 2nd Lieutenant
O'Brien, William, 2nd Lieutenant

Fitch, H.S., 1st Sergeant
Davis, Josephus, 2nd Sergeant
Beeler, Louis F., 3rd Sergeant
Adams, John H., 4th Sergeant

Stockton, Lewis F., Corporal
Dobbin, William, Corporal
Wild, Thomas, Corporal
Fultz, George S., Corporal

Woodfield, Joseph, Musician

Privates
Andlum, John
Beall, William
Brown, Charles P.
Brown, Allen
Burton, Abner
Chipps, David
Carroll, William
Dungan, Henry
Donally, John
Dement, William E.
Dick, Peter
Eld, Henry
Gibson, William
Genty, Antonia
Hill, George

Hurdle, Jackson
Hurt, Barney
Houssanstopp, John
Heyn, Henry
Hindmans, William
Hiver, John
Jones, Jacob
Kimp, Andrew
Knott, Joseph
Luxson, Joseph
Longerback, Frederick
Lawrence, George
Liles, William
Morrow, Henry A.
Mount, Thomas
McLaughlin, John

McPherson, William
Milstead, William
Pingle, Henry
Peastner, William
Rank, Joseph
Steward, George
Sprigg, William
Tyler, George
Vail, Rowen
Woodward, William A.
Coady, Francis
Emory, Lewis
Stiner, Daniel
Storm, John

Company D: Baltimore and District of Columbia Volunteers Battalion

Waters, John, Captain
Boyle, Eugene, Captain
Schaeffer, Francis B., Captain

Parham, William J., 1st Lieutenant
Murphy, Edward, 2nd Lieutenant

Ingle, Henry, 1st Sergeant
Hantner, John, 2nd Sergeant
Gassaway, Madison, 3rd Sergeant
Judd, George F., 4th Sergeant

Fitzgerald, Thomas, Corporal
Pierce, John, Corporal
Ruly, Joseph, Corporal
Boswell, Thomas B., Corporal
Pool, Lewis, Musician

Privates
Barry, Daniel
Brown, Thomas
Cover, Daniel
Cross, Thomas
Cockran, James
Cooper, James A.
Coady, Francis
Dwyer, Thomas
Darley, John W.
Fasnaught, George
Goddard, Calvin

Johns, Walter
Jackson, Samuel A.
Joyce, John T.
Kelly, Thaddius
Knight, Henry
King, Thomas
Lewis, William
Moran, James
Martin, James
Noah, Stinch.
Norris, Andrew J.
Ogden, John

Payne, John
Richardson, John
Robinson, Henry P.
Simpson, John F.
Stevenson, John
Thomas, William
Taylor, John
Tolson, Douglas
Vermillion, Charles
Wills, John
Weeks, William H.
Yeck, Charles

Company E: Baltimore and District of Columiba Volunteers Battalion

Kenly, John R., Commanding Officer, Captain

Schaeffer, Francis B., 1st Lieutenant
Bowie, Oden, 2nd Lieutenant

Aisquith, William E., Sergeant
Hickman, William, Sergeant
Lansdale, George Oliver, Sergeant
Tyser, Thomas, Sergeant

Brand, Benjamin F., Corporal
Mansfield, James H., Corporal
Beacham, James A., Corporal
Tibbles, James, Corporal
Creamer, John, Corporal

Privates
Andrews, John
Alexander, John F.
Allen, John
Allen, William
Atkinson, Lemuel
Bowie, George W.
Billington, John A.
Butler, William A.
Bannister, William
Beaston, Samuel
Boyd, John
Boulanger, Edward
Baker, Jacob
Byram, Edward I.
Belt, Richard H.
Canning, James B.
Collins, George N.
Cutting, DeAzro A.B.
Degomp, Jacob
Dobbin, Francis M.
Dick, Joseph H.
Elting, Henry J.
Fischer, Charles
Fuller, Louis
Forbush, Henry
Fisher, Francis
Gordon, George
Gelston, Samuel

Henxler, Vincent
Hisskins, John H.
Henry, James
Hawkins, Barney
Hugo, George T.
Hill, Charles
Healey, George
Hatch, William S.
Heft, Henry
Herdenback, Charles
Johnson, Charles
Johnson, John S.
Johnson, David
Knight, Leroy
Leyburn, Thomas
Leventon, Thomas
Labedie, Francis A.
Loughry, John
Lockhart, Samuel
Macready, William
Macnelly, George
Millard, Joseph B.
Merton, James H.
Morris, Jacob
Magness, John
Matchett, Charles W.
McGunnell, John
Myers, Edward
Norris, Henry P.

Nettan, Francis Louis
Nimocks, Franklin B.
Pregg, Josiah
Pratt, Charles
Peregoy, James
Rogers, Seth S.
Reese, John
Richardson, Joseph B.
Riley, William M.S.
Ritter, Andrew I.
Rapley, William
Robinson, John K.
Sullivan, James W.
Smith, John
Stansbury, Thomas T.
Sibley, William H.
Turner, John W.
Wharry, Joseph
Williams, Daniel
Wilson, William
Tressel, Ernest

Mustered in at a later time:
Creamer, John
Henderson, Armistead
Ramsay, Alexander
Heft, Henry
Heidelbach, Charles

Company F: Baltimore and District of Columbia Volunteers Battalion

Boyd, James, Captain - Baltimore

Ruddach, Joseph H., 1st Lieutenant - Baltimore
Haslett, Robert E., 2nd Lieutenant - Baltimore
Taneyhill, James, 3rd Lieutenant - Baltimore

Rider, John W., 1st Sergeant - Baltimore
Axer, John, 2nd Sergeant - Baltimore
Alden, John, 3rd Sergeant - Baltimore
Posey, John P., 4th Sergeant - Baltimore
Ehrman, Charles H., Sergeant

Rochester, George, 1st Corporal - Baltimore
Stephenson, Edward W., 2nd Corporal - Baltimore
McIntire, James H., 3rd Corporal - Baltimore
Robey, William, 4th Corporal - Baltimore
Duncan, Louis, Corporal
Whitcomb, Otis Jr., Corporal

Privates

Allen, John E. - Baltimore
Boyd, James
Barker, Samuel P.
Busey, James R.
Boyd, William
Boyer, William
Coupland, William G.
Craddock, William H.
Crough, John S.
Fitzpatrick, Owen
Glass, Thomas
Gifford, Henry
Hands, Lafayette
Henry, John D.
Harrison, John D.
Hope, Thomas
Herman, Michael
Jackson, Clarence
Kline, Godfrey
Lovell, William
Lane, Michael
Lawn, John
Mallory, Wallace F.
Mahone, Roger J.
Meteer, Andrew
Nock, William
Preston, John
Plummer, James H.
Robinson, William

Rusk, James
Steuart, Charles B.
Small, James
Search, Edwin K.
Seim, Charles
Stone, Melvin S.
Shillonn, Joseph P.
Thomas, George H.
Tuttle, Charles
Vernon, William
Wagner, James E.
Wingate, Thomas J.
Wolf, Louis
Woods, John
Weeks, William H.
Wood, William H.
Wilson, James
Young, William
Hamilton, John
Brown, Basil
Green, George
Gardner, James
Klassen, Jacob
Mearis, Leonard
Wells, Daniel
Kane, Robert
Plowman, Alfred
Hanlan, Richard
Kelly, William
Pearson, George W.
Wicker, Jacob

Herring, George A.
Anderson, Thomas J.
Allen, James H.
Brown, Basil P.
Dickson, George P.
Fleurix, James M.
Finlay, John
Gardner, John
Gaddess, Alexander Jr.
Gillingham, Horace H.
Greene, George G.
Gardner, James F.
Haslet, James
Herring, George A.
Hanlon, Richard
Hamilton, John W.
Heckrotte, Henry W.
Worrell, William
McNeal, William
McKeldin, David W.
McMackin, Robert
Robisson, Samuel O.
Smith, John B.
Scott, William A.
Schieck, John P.
Summers, George
Tuthill, David M.
White, George W.
Morrell, Edward

MUSTER ROLL FOR THE MARYLAND AND DISTRICT OF COLUMBIA REGIMENT

Regimental Staff

Hughes, George W., Commanding Officer, Colonel

Emory, William H., Lt. Colonel
Kenly, John R., Major
Steele, James, Adjutant
Cororan, William, A.A.G.M.V.
Tilghman, Stedman R., Surgeon
Bryerly, Wakeman, Asst. Surgeon

Brannan, John, Sgt. Major
Purdon, John, G.M. Sgt.

Company A: Maryland and District Volunteers Regiment

Degges, William H., Captain

Addison, Henry S., 1st Lieutenant
Ballman, John H., 2nd Lieutenant
Dowden, Raymond P., 2nd Lieutenant

Glover, John W., 1st Sergeant
Nally, William H., 2nd Sergeant
Laugton, Samuel W., 3rd Sergeant
Reeve, William, 4th Sergeant

Penn, Thomas, 1st Corporal
Jackson, John W., 2nd Corporal
Bender, Jacob A., 3rd Corporal

Privates

Bailey, James
Baker, Charles F.
Beam, J. Hileary
Brown, Addison
Brown, John
Coe, Robert
Colb, Frederick
Cornwell, Benson
Curry, David
Clark, Robert
Carroll, William
Deakins, John
Elflin, George
Eahe, Henry
Finnegan, Peter
Fisher, Henry
Garrison, Bartlett
Gates, William J.
Gitner, Philip
Gier, Christopher
Hagedorn, Frederick
Hilliary, John C.
Howe, Edward
Johnson, Francis
Jordan, John
Kelly, John
Katzenberger, John
Kammera, Henry
Lanham, Jonathan
Luidie, Henry B.
Markam, Francis
Moller, Nicholas
Macbeth, John
Miller, Henry
Magruder, Gabriel
McGreggor, John J.
Penn, Jacob W.
Reyner, Samuel
Rawlings, James
Reichter, John
Reinlein, John
Robbins, Patrick
Rickmarr, Frederick
Schneider, George J. Leo
Schraick, Nicholas
Schron, Frederick
Schwalbe, John P.
Seizd, Frederick
Smith, Frederick
Tucker, Charles H.
Vogle, Valentine
Watkins, Nicholas
Wyner, Henry

Company B: Maryland and District Volunteers Regiment

Barry, Edmund, Captain

Thornton, John M., 1st Lieutenant
Carr, John, 2nd Lieutenant
Geary, William J., 2nd Lieutenant

Thompson, John H., 1st Sergeant
Wallis, Edward L., Sergeant
Rheim, George, Sergeant
Purdon, John, 2nd Sergeant

Milbourn, Timothy, Corporal
Day, John, Corporal
Dolson, Vernon, Corporal
Hutchinson, William, Corporal

Young, Thomas, Musician
Drisey, Francis, Musician

MUSTER ROLL FOR THE MARYLAND AND D.C. REGIMENT

Privates
Beach, William
Bean, Josiah
Bush, James William
Bush, William S.
Butler, David
Clark, Samie T.
Clemments, Dominick
Conner, James
Cowen, Thomas
Cresman, Michael
Derr, John
Dolan, William
Dorsey, Francis Q.
Downy, Hugh
Drudge, George
Drudge, William
Duncan, Thomas
Eslinger, Christian
Fergi, J.
Fowler, Jesse
Gammitt, Thomas

Gardner, George T.
Gibson, George T.
Glover, Edward R.
Grey, Anthony
Grey, Nathaniel
Grimes, John
Hanison, Richard
Haxton, Columbus E.
Hoff, Henry
Holen, Daniel H.
Hart, George
Lewis, Edward
Myer, George
Myers, Charles F. H.
McCoy, William
McDonald, James A.
McLaughlin, Thomas
McNaughton, Samuel
Moran, John
Moran, Thomas
Myerhoffer, Peter
Nimmocks, Leonard

Osbourn, John
Palmer, William
Parsons, Joseph
Phacf, John M.
Quigley, Edward
Rowlett, Edward
Rupter, Joseph
Salisbury, John
Shafer, Henry
Shorter, George
Shineburger, Christopher
Slount, Winslow
Thompson, Benjamin T.
Tissfrits, Samuel
Watts, James
White, Charles
Willett, Francis
Witney, Charles
Wolf, Samuel
Young, N.

Company C: Maryland and District of Columbia Volunteers Regiment

Dolan, Lawrence, Captain

Hooper, John, 1st Lieutenant
Mabbett, Ira, 2nd Lieutenant
Bell, Robert C., 2nd Lieutenant

Bell, William, 1st Sergeant
Carr, William, 2nd Sergeant
Bowers, George, 3rd Sergeant
Kraft, Edward B., 4th Sergeant

Armstrong, Robert, 1st Corporal
Powell, George W., 2nd Corporal
Berger, Jacob, 3rd Corporal
Neidhamer, John, 4th Corporal

Frederick, Frank, Musician

Privates
Anderman, Frederick
Armstrong, George
Bromslea, Henry
Blakenoy, Samuel
Buckhaus, David
Deckard, John
Degomp, Jacob
Deckard, Jacob C.
Fury, John G.
Gerborth, Christian
Hackett, George W.
Hubner, Frederick
Hasselman, Taleman

James, George
Kounselman, Frederick
Kloman, Charles
Kasting, Augustus
Kastine, Harman
McPolan, Thomas
Monroe, John
Murphy, Daniel
Myer, John
Norherman, Henry B.
Owens, David
Pindle, William
Smith, Alexander N.
Swan, George E.

Scott, James
Slear, Christopher
Shula, John J.
Sesselman, John
Sharer, William C.
Swaits, Joseph
Traverse, Tolerance J.
Talbot, Jeremiah
West, James W.
Welch, Ephraim
Wilson, Robert
Wenholn, Frederick
Wright, Joshua
Wherler, Nathaniel
Yeitman, John

86   MARYLAND AND D.C. VOLUNTEERS IN THE MEXICAN WAR

Company D: Maryland and District of Columbia Volunteers Regiment

Henrie, Dan Drake, Captain

Klopfer, Frederick A., 1st Lieutenant
West, Benjamin R., 2nd Lieutenant
Henry, Richard P., 2nd Lieutenant

Burns, Benjamin F., 1st Sergeant
Halderman, Jacob M., 2nd Sergeant
Bowen, Alexander H., 3rd Sergeant
Forrest, David C., 4th Sergeant

Locke, John H., Corporal
Gorman, William, Corporal

Jones, Alfred, Musician
Sloan, William H., Musician

Privates
Appleby, Ridgely
Bacon, Joseph K.
Birch, John D.
Brooks, William H.
Barbour, Washington T.
Clarke, Marcellus
Clemmens, Christopher C.
Cook, Mason G.
Floyd, Albion K.P.
Finnegan, Phillip
Gife, Edward
Gorman, James
Gurner, Auguste

Hardy, George
Harwood, Alexander H.
Johnson, William
Keenan, John F.
Keenan, Thomas
Lockhears, Josiah
Magee, William
McBrafly, John
McConnell, John
McGinly, John
Miller, Jacob G.
Misler, Josiah
Moore, John
Murray, Rufus
O'Keefe, Francis B.

Pease, William H.
Ressing, William
Robinson, Levi H.
Rombollz, John G.
Sandford, Lynas
Spalding, George
Taylor, Samuel
Tucker, William W.
Watson, Justice
Weiland, George C.
Welters, James
Wood, Thomas W.
Walker, James D.
Wilson, Lancelot

Company E: Maryland and District of Columbia Regiment

Brown, George W., Captain
Hopper, Washington, 1st Lieutenant
O'Brien, James, 2nd Lieutenant
Gronewell, John H.. 2nd Lieutenant

Chambers, John Thomas, 1st Sergeant
Smith, Y.J.W., 2nd Sergeant
Alexander, John J., 3rd Sergeant
Gantt, Nicholas B., 4th Sergeant

Jarvis, Robert B., 1st Corporal
Wilson, William H., 2nd Corporal
Welch, John B., 3rd Corporal
Gordon, Josias B., 4th Corporal

Galloway, John T.H., Drummer

Privates
Baney, William
Beck, George
Bell, William
Brazier, John W.
Clark, William
Clark, John
Clark, George
Clark, John A.
Caster, Thomas
Caster, Joseph
Camper, Frances
Cole, Frances
Connelly, James
Cockran, Patrick
Camsten, Joseph
Dise, John
Egan, John Thomas

Fish, John
Fitzsimmons, John
Foster, William
Flood, William
Fornshill, James
Fordenburg, John
Goerl, Samuel
Gewette, Earnest
Hax, Henry
Hax, Peter
Heyer, Frederick
Hobbs, Beau H.
Hoffman, John H.
Horn, John
Holt, John W.
Haupp, Casper
Hutchings, William
Jacobs, William

Jarrette, William J.
Jones, John
Kauffman, Nicholas
Kendall, Charles
Knight, James
Knimick, John
Kock, Martin
Kraft, William
Kenny, John
Kenny, Mathew
Ledoger, John B.
Link, William B.
Ludwig, Francis
Lewscomb, Jacob
Lauman, Josias
McCormick, John
Mead, Patrick
Martin, John

MUSTER ROLL FOR THE MARYLAND AND D.C. REGIMENT

Oneil, James
Pyle, Joseph
Parkhill, Hamilton
Polly, Thomas
Pierpoint, John
Pierpoint, Amoss
Quigley, Robert
Ramsey, James
Rawlings, William

Reeder, John
Riley, Daniel
Ross, Charles C.
Schmidt, Valentine
Schaffer, Simon
Slicker, Samuel
Stout, Frances
Sinton, Thomas J.
Tierney, James

Turner, Robert
Wagner, Henry
Walker, Robert L.
Wolfe, George
Weaver, John
Wingate, William h.
Ward, Daniel

Company F: Maryland and District of Columbia Volunteers Regiment

Taylor, Marcellus K., Captain

Klassen, Jacob S., 1st Lieutenant
Baker, William H., 2nd Lieutenant
Steel, James, 2nd Lieutenant

Wright, John, 1st Sergeant
Bartting, Thomas, 2nd Sergeant
Stewart, William, 3rd Sergeant
Ehrman, Charles H., 4th Sergeant

Todd, George W., 1st Corporal
McClane, George W., 2nd Corporal
Murdoch, Gilbert, 3rd Corporal
Hogan, William, 4th Corporal

Bradly, James, Musician

Privates
Anderson, Thomas
Aydelott, Benjamin
Alderdiks, John
Arthur, John
Baker, Henry J.
Barclay, James
Bennett, George W.
Bomberger, John H.
Barthold, Christian
Brown, William
Burnham, James
Butler, David
Biddle, Richard
Buckers, John
Corey, Nicholas
Clifford, William
Collins, George
Doyle, Samuel B.
Dungan, Alexander
Edwards, Joseph
Gorman, Patrick
Graham, James
Guy, James

Green, Daniel
Haggerty, George W.
Hunter, Adam M.
Hurley, George W.
Irving, James
Josephs, Abram
Johnson, Mathew
Johnson, William
Kelly, Thomas
Kennedy, George W.
Kidd, William P.
Loyd, John
McCain, James
Mannion, Joseph
Mason, Edward W.
Morse, Augustus T.
Miller, Edward
McLaughlin, James
Murray, Frank J.
Nichols, William
Pim, John P.
Perdue, John
Reynolds, Charles A.
Rose, Robert

Riley, John H.
Roberts, John
Smith, Hugh
Smith, Robert
Sharion, Patrick
Shoek, Samuel
Stedrens, William R.
Stits, William
Stewart, John
Stewart, John N.
Talbot, Nicholas B.
Tamrez, Joseph
Thompson, Alexander
Willard, Daniel
Wilson, Thomas
Webster, Joshua W.
Webb, Daniel C.
Weber, Alexander
Wayson, James
Welch, James
Wilson, Joseph W.
Greenwood, Charles H.

88   MARYLAND AND D.C. VOLUNTEERS IN THE MEXICAN WAR

Company G (Light Artillery): Maryland and District of Columbia Volunteers Regiment

Tilghman, Lloyd, Captain

Morrow, Isaac H., 1st Lieutenant
Tensfield, Arnold, 2nd Lieutenant
Milnor, Henry M., 2nd Lieutenant
Tilghman, Frisbie, 1st Lieutenant

Petherbridge, C.R., 1st Sergeant
Murray, David G., 2nd Sergeant
Purcell, Charles W., 3rd Sergeant
Schnell, Andrew R., 4th Sergeant

Wilby, Charles C., 1st Corporal
Matthews, John H., 2nd Corporal

Kennedy, William B., 3rd Corporal
Swift, Charles, 4th Corporal

Foust, John, Artificer
McElwee, William, Artificer

Rodgers, Alexander H., Chief Musician

Privates
Armstrong, James
Ackenback, John
Barnard, John H.
Bennett, Davis
Billington, G. S.
Boss, Isaac
Clements, James
Cooley, Edward
Christopher, John
Cline, George
Carraw, James
Chambers, Benjamin F.
Day, Samuel
Daushady, Richard
Finlay, William H.
Goodrich, Thomas J.
Gile, Edward
Ham, Anthony
Haugh, Benjamin B.
Hunter, R.
Harris, James
Knott, Walter D.
Krust, Thomas
Lickey, James
Luson, Morrison
Lane, Charles
Lovell, George
Lee, Edward
Meeks, Allen
McCeeny, Zacharia
Moore, J.M.
McCormick, William
Mitchell, George
McGee, Daniel
Moran, A.F.
McKenzie, William

McMarr, John
Mills, Thomas
Norwood, John
O'Mealley, Thomas
Pactoleto, Lorant
Porter, Edward P.
Rosenburg, Edward
Reely, Artemus
Reynolds, James
Robinson, Henry
Simpson, Ezeikiel
Simpson, C.D.
Short, Isaac
Surghnor, Thompson
Sevan, Osborn C.
Tolbert, John
Taylor, William
Traynor, James
Titlow, John
Vernon, Patrick
Warren, William F.
Wood, Andrew J.
Waters, Peter
Walsh, James
Wyman, Henry
Weems, William M.
Wilson, John
Webster, Henry W.
Thompson, John
Martine, George
Keller, Charles
Manning, Martin
Jerrard, Owen
Hughes, Anthony
Forsyth, William A.
Graham, John
Love, John A.

Williams, Henry
Boss, Anthony
Ball, John
Freed, George K.
Hassell, William F.
Gregory, James
Buckley, James
Kreamer, George
Boyle, Henry
Miller, Edward
Kernin, Joseph
Sharkey, John
McEnroe, James
Jones, G.R.
Cook, William B.
Troxall, David M.
Broadus, Edward
Crown, Francis
Huxford, Thomas J.
Turner, George A.
Cook, Robert
Kelly, James
Kelly, John
Hilbert, Henry
Stayton, William
Pease, William
Wallace, Patrick
Othick, Henry
Bolkman, Frederick
Volandt, J.C.F.
Young, William
Young, ?. H.
Tensfield, John
Nicholson, E.J.
Bares, John T.
Parras, Joseph

MUSTER ROLL FOR THE MARYLAND AND D.C. REGIMENT

Company H: Maryland and District of Columbia Volunteers Regiment

Schaeffer, Francis B., Captain

Corcoran, William J., 1st Lieutenant
Griffith, David A., 2nd Lieutenant
Mulloy, John J., 2nd Lieutenant

Ingle, Henry, 1st Sergeant
Mansfield, James H., 2nd Sergeant
Brandall, Joseph, 3rd Sergeant
Woods, William H., 4th Sergeant

King, Thomas, 1st Corporal
Barker, Samuel A., 2nd Corporal
Manning, Thomas, 3rd Corporal
Davis, Ludwell H., 4th Corporal

Privates
Anderson, Jesse
Anderson, John R.
Anderson, Aquilla
Alden, John
Bauff, Henry
Bauff, John
Berry, Thomas
Boswell, Thomas P.
Beale, William H.
Brown, Bassel
Brown, John
Barozy, Paul
Castleman, Nath'l G.
Cochran, James
Cook, William
Connolly, Edward
Cripps, John F.
Dermidy, Walter
Edmonson, Nathan
Edwards, Thomas W.
Fagan
Fairall, Alfred

Fisher, John T.
Goddard, Calvin
Griffith, Edward
Gayhart, Joseph
Gordon, Nathaniel
Grumble, James
Green, Noah
Hatch, Julius
Harrison, William H.
Hennrick, Jacob C.
Hughes, Thomas W.
Jarvin, Washington H.
Jenkins, John J.
Jordan, John
Keife, James
Krebs, James
Kelly, Jackson
Kump, Joseph
Kuntz, Thomas
Leitch, Andrew J.
Lancaster, George W.
Lennox, William
Lloyd, Joshua

Moran, John
Minnick, William
Miffitt, Joseph
Nibling, Henry
Page, William
Payne, Elisha R.
Reeder, John F.
Rider, George W.
Reeves, Hazekiah
Russell, Andrew S.
Swartz, Augustine
Snyder, John A.
Scattergood, John G.
Stansbury, Edward H.
Severe, Francis F.
Stephens, Thomas W.
Trippard, James B.
Talbot, George
Turner, Robert
Walden, James
Wallack, Robb
Wingate, Thomas
Woodward, Henry P.

Recruiting Party

Mabbitt, Ira, Commander, 2nd Lieutenant

Crone, William, Pvt.
Crone, Robert H., Pvt.
Cleggett, Otho, Pvt.
Howe, A.L., Pvt.
Hanna, Lawrence, Pvt.
Kendig, Benjamin F., Pvt.
Love, John A., Pvt.
Thayre, Stephen, Pvt.

Cunin, Samuel, Pvt.
Cleary, James, Pvt.
Lucas, Thomas, Pvt.
Turner, Joshua, Pvt.

Bibliography

Books

Bill, Alfred H. <u>Rehearsal for Conflict: The War With Mexico, 1846-1848.</u> New York: Alfred A. Knopf, 1947.

DuFour, Charles L. <u>The Mexican War.</u> New York: Hawthorn Books, 1968.

Eisenhower, John S.D. <u>So Far From God: The U.S. War with Mexico 1846—1848.</u> New York: Doubleday, 1989.

Frost, J. <u>The Mexican War and Its Warriors.</u> Philadephia: H. Mansfield, 1850.

<u>General Taylor and His Staff.</u> Philadelphia: Grigg, Elliot & Co., 1848.

<u>History of Baltimore, Maryland.</u> Baltimore: S.B. Nelson, 1898.

Kenly, John R. <u>Memoirs of a Maryland Volunteer.</u> Philadelphia: J.B. Lippincott & Co., 1873.

McIntosh, James, et.al., editors. <u>The Papers of Jefferson Davis.</u> Baton Rouge: Louisiana State University Press, 1981.

Nichols, Edward J. <u>Zach Taylor's Little Army.</u> Garden City, N.Y.: Doubleday, 1963.

Peterson, Clarence S. <u>Known Military Dead During the Mexican War, 1846—1848.</u> Baltimore, 1957.

Powell, Henry F. *Tercentenary History of Maryland.* Chicago: S.J. Clarke Publishing Co., 1925.

Proctor, John C., editor. *Washington: Past and Present: A History.* New York: Lewis Historical Publishing Co., 1930.

Reid, Samuel C. *The Scouting Expeditions of McCulloch's Texas Rangers.* Freeport, N.Y.: Books for Libraries Press, 1970 (reprint).

Ripley, R.S. *The War With Mexico.* New York: B. Franklin, 1970 (reprint>.

Scharf, J. Thomas. *History of Baltimore City and County, Maryland.* Philadelphia: Louis H. Everts, 1881.

Scharf, J. Thomas. *The Chronicles of Baltimore.* Baltimore: Turnbull Brothers, 1874.

Sifakis, Stewart. *Who Was Who in the Union.* New York: Facts on File, 1988.

Singletary, Otis A. *The Mexican War.* Chicago: University of ChicagoPress, 1960.

Slauson, Allan, editor. *A History of the City of Washington: Its Men and Institutions.* Washington: Washington Post Co., 1903.

Smith, Justin H. *The War With Mexico.* Gloucester, Mass. : P. Smith, 1963 (reprint).

The Biographical Cyclopedia of Representative Men of Maryland and D.C. Baltimore: National Biographical Publishing Co., 1879.

Time-Life Books. The Mexican War. Alexandria, Va.: Time-Life Books, 1978.

Wilcox, Cadmus M. History of the Mexican War. Washington: The Church News Publishing Co., 1892.

Newspapers and Periodicals

Annapolis Star. May 28, 1846.

Backus, Electus. "A Brief Sketch of the Battle of Monterey; With Details . . . ," Historical Magazine. July, 1866.

Baltimore American. May 20, 23, 1846, Nov. 30, 1878

Baltimore Sun. May 19—21, 23, 1846, June 1, 1846, July 21, 1846, October 12, 16, 17, 21, 1846. May 20, 1847, June 11, 1847, Sept. 22, 1882

Baltimore Sunday Herald. June 28, 1903.

Daily National Intelligencer. May 20, 1846.

Daily Republican Argus. October 17, 1846.

Other Sources

Baltimore City Archives, Membership of the Association of Veterans of the Mexican War.

Chicago Historical Society, Lloyd Tilghman Collection.

Johns, Henry Rev. *A Sermon on Sunday, January 19, 1847.*
Baltimore: I.O.O.F., 1847.

Maryland Historical Society, Manuscripts: 159, 2674, 1902, 507.

Topham, Washington. "The Old Globe Offices and the Publishers," *Records of the Columbia Historical Society.* Washington, D.C. Columbia Historical Society, 1935.

United States Congress. *Executive Document Number 4.* Washington: United States House of Representatives, 2nd Session, 29th Congress

www.ingramcontent.com/pod-product-compliance
Lightning Source LLC
Chambersburg PA
CBHW070306100426
42743CB00011B/2369